The adventures of a woman called by God and transformed by the people she meets in the far places of the earth.

NIGHT JOURNEYS

RAYLENE PEARCE

Ark House Press
PO Box 1722, Port Orchard, WA 98366 USA
PO Box 1321, Mona Vale NSW 1660 Australia
PO Box 318 334, West Harbour, Auckland 0661 New Zealand
arkhousepress.com

© 2016 Raylene Pearce

All rights reserved. No part of this publication may be reproduced, stored in a retrieval system or transmitted in any form or by any means, electronic, mechanical, photocopying, recording or otherwise, without the prior written permission of the publisher.

The information, views, opinions and visuals expressed in this publication are solely those of the author and does not reflect those of the publisher. The publisher disclaims any liabilities or responsibilities whatsoever for any damages, libel or liabilities arising directly or indirectly from the contents of this publication.

A copy of this publication can be found in the National Library of Australia. All rights reserved. No part of this publication may be reproduced, stored in a retrieval system or transmitted in any form or by any means electronic, mechanical, photocopying, recording or otherwise without the prior written permission of the publisher.
Scripture Quotations are taken from The Holy Bible, New International Version - (unless otherwise noted in the text)
International Bible Society, 1820 Jet Stream Drive, Colorado Springs CO 80921-3696

Cataloguing in Publication Data:
Title: Night Journeys
ISBN: 9780648291497 (pbk.)
Subjects: Memoirs, Biography
Other Authors/Contributors: Pearce, Raylene
Author photo taken by Kelsey Grace Photography
Internal photos, by the author, James Winter, Norm Tucker & Grieg Kidman.
Design and layout by initiateagency.com

This book recounts events in the life of Raylene Pearce according to the author's recollection and from the author's perspective. Some dialogue and certain other details have been altered for purposes of the author's narrative. Although Raylene has done everything in her power to check facts, she cannot verify the accuracy of every detail contained within these pages. Many names of people, places and companies have been changed. This is a work of creative non-fiction. All mistakes are hers.

Foreword

I walk across the railway bridge. It's crowded with people coming off trains south from Cairo and north from Helwan. I approach the office and to my surprise I see all the staff out on the street. Some of the women run towards me and I can see they are agitated.

'What's wrong?' I ask.

'Didn't you feel the earthquake? It was huge, the building swayed and books fell out of shelves and —'

I interrupt Sonya. 'I didn't feel any earthquake. I was on the bridge. It always moves. I didn't feel anything! What a bummer, now I haven't anything to write home about!'

They look at me, shocked at my callousness.

'I've just rung my husband,' says Rania. 'He's in Alexandria and all the produce fell off the shelves in the shop he was visiting.'

'Yes,' says Sonya, whose three German Shepherds live on the twenty-sixth floor with her and her husband. 'My dogs will be so upset. I must go to them.'

And she hails a taxi there and then and disappears towards Heliopolis.

****

The mantra I chanted throughout the decade
I lived in the Middle East,
as things got tough,
when plans went awry, was:
'This will make a great story.
This is something to write home about.'
And write I did.

And I called my stories *'Night Journeys'*.

Night Journeys

****

This memoir includes scenes from my childhood, but from 1994 to 2004 while I lived in the Middle East, I wrote to my team supporters officially four times a year and I sent frequent emails. These years are mainly a re-write of four box-files full of a neatly filed history of me between plastic sleeves.

A Special Appreciation

'Why is there a thorn in your thumb?'

'I don't know.'

Dorothy has been praying for me and she sees a picture in her mind of a thumb with a thorn in it.

'Were you ever put down by anyone in relation to writing?'

'Yes. Everything I wrote as a child at school was covered in red marks because I was a bad speller, or creative, if you looked at it another way. I could spell one word many ways, but that was not appreciated, and I was told I was dumb by my teachers.'

'Have you ever forgiven them?'

'Haven't thought about it.'

'What do you think the thorn in your thumb means?'

'I don't know, except that a thorn in my thumb might stop me writing.'

'I think so too. Let's pray about that now. I can pray release from any put-down from the past, so that you can write for the future.'

****

During the 1980's I completed a Creative Living Course at Tabor College Adelaide taken by Barry Chant, and at the end of the course the question was asked, 'What next?'

My answer was, 'I want to write.'

Something was stopping me from doing a 'Writing for the Media' course at Adelaide TAFE. So here we were praying about this.

To encourage me, Dorothy said that when I got published I was to acknowledge her. I noticed that she didn't say 'if' I got published!

The outcome of that prayer was that I became a student at The Bible College of South Australia, passed exams from The Australian

College of Divinity, and studied various writing subjects at Adelaide TAFE. While in Egypt I wrote extensively for the Magazine as the English Language Editor and created other projects that were translated into Arabic. On return from Egypt in 2005 I studied at Flinders University and gained a Bachelor of Arts in Creative Writing in 2009. And have now written this book.

I thank God for Dorothy O'Neill.

Acknowledgements

I acknowledge you, the reader. I hope that you will find, as you read this memoir, that I am speaking to you as if we were sitting in the same room. Or perhaps, if you prefer, a little more distant as part of an audience, when I'm on a speaking tour. I'm praying that as you engage in this book, you will be challenged out of being a spectator to becoming a participator. That's what Jesus did when he left the Community of the God Head and became one of us – living our life, dying our death, and living again for and with us for eternity.

Many personal names and organizational names have been changed for security reasons. My seconding agency will be known as *The Company* for this book.

I want to celebrate, here, the countless people who put their faith in Jesus because of the work of Christian media – through television, radio, films, children's cartoons, magazines, books and satellite broadcasts in many languages. Throughout the Middle East mobile phones and the internet have opened up former 'closed countries' to the Good News, facilitated by dedicated people on the ground.

It was into this area of ministry that I was seconded.

****

Commendation

It was John Stott who said that the most fascinating biographies are not those that merely tell someone's story, but those that uncover the writer's secret – the driving force of her life. Well, Raylene's secret is out; though if you know Raylene, her secret would have been evident from the moment you met.

Raylene has laid bare what makes her "tick": her passion for God, for people and for adventure. Even a hole in a Cairo road is adventure to Raylene! She traces her spirited childhood through to a teenage call from God on her life; to the pain of losing her 52 year old mother, her beloved Nanna and her first marriage; to rearing two sons on a part-time mission salary; to a previously unimagined life for God among peoples of other cultures and other faiths on the other side of the world.

Raylene was freed to express her desires: to dance in the aisles, to connect her Celtic faith ancestry with the Copts of Egypt, to walk in the footsteps of Moses on Mt Sinai, and to love for Jesus' sake those who've never heard.

University studies at the age of 60 and the further gift of a desire of her heart, a wonderful husband, have led her further into pouring her life into the lives of others, a story yet to be completed.

This book reveals God's utter faithfulness in the big and the small in the journey of a self-confessed adventurous, sometimes-naïve, passionate woman of God.

An engaging read!

Berys Nixon was the Personnel Director: *The Company* (Australia) during Raylene's tenure, 1983 - 2005 except for the final years when Berys worked in Central Asia.

****

Contents

PART ONE: EGYPT & INDIA   xx
  1 Surprise Encounter – Egypt (2002)   xx
  2 The Girl on a Night Journey – India (1991)   09

PART TWO: SOUTH AUSTRALIA   11
  3 Growing Character – South Australia (1946)   13
  4 Into Bed with Nanna (1952)   21
  5 Direction at Last (1959 – 1962)   25
  6 Memorial Memories – (1963-1967)   30
  7 Night of Storms (1968)   35
  8 Hibiscus (1972)   39
  9 Night Sea Journey – PNG (1980-82)   50
  10 Shame Suffering (1983)   56
  11 Nanna and the Good Shepherd (1987)   59
  12 The Tale of Two Houses (1983-1988)   62
  13 The Old Stove (1993)   68

PART THREE: ASIA   73
  14 Tears of the Women – Thailand (1986)   75
  15 Hospitality – Nepal (1991)   78
  16 Night Journey to Pokhara (1991)   81
  17 India Experiences (1991)   86
  18 The Gorakhpur Station Ladies' Waiting Room (1991)   88
  19 Night Journey to Delhi (1991)   92
  20 Flying Solo – Australia & Cyprus (1994)   95

PART FOUR: CYPRUS — 99
21 Island in the Sun (1994) — 101
22 Divided Life (1994) — 104
23 Methuselah and Me (1995) — 110
24 Never go North (1995) — 114
25 Blacklisted (1995) — 117

PART FIVE: OFF ISLAND — 121
26 Connections, Connections, Connections: (1995-1999) — 123
27 Making Connections – Germany (1996) — 128
28 Making More Connections – Cornwall UK (1996) — 131
29 Two days in the life of an Aussie Traveller UK (1990) — 139
30 Planes, Trains and still going the Wrong Way! To the ends of the Earth (1990's) — 144
31 Lindisfarne Island – UK (2002) — 147
32 Connecting Again – UK (1996) — 156

PART SIX: EGYPT — 161
33 Burps in the Night (1994) — 163
34 Still Mediterranean Hopping (1996) — 169
35 Hot Cairo Night (1998) — 174
36 Night Desert Ride & Consequences (1999) — 178
37 Sabry and his Sisters (1999) — 185
38 Invalid & Fayoum (2000) — 190
39 Women in Print (2000) — 195
40 Mentioning More Men (2000's) — 203
41 Eid el Adha (2003) — 208
42 The Tale of Two Theatres (2003) — 218
43 Holy, Holy, Holy: Holy Water & Holy Man (2000's) — 222

44 Holy Mountain (2000's)	228
45 Everything Changes (2001)	236
46 New World, New Flat, New Friends (2001)	245
47 Raining in Egypt (2001)	254
48 Back to the Future – (2001, 2003 & 2015)	261
PART SEVEN: REVERSE CULTURE SHOCK	267
49 Whachyorname? – Egypt (2004) Footpaths – (2005)	269
50 Home at Last (2005)	279
Afterword – The Icing on the Cake	281
Further Acknowledgements	288
How To Support Project Kola	291
About the Author	293

Part One

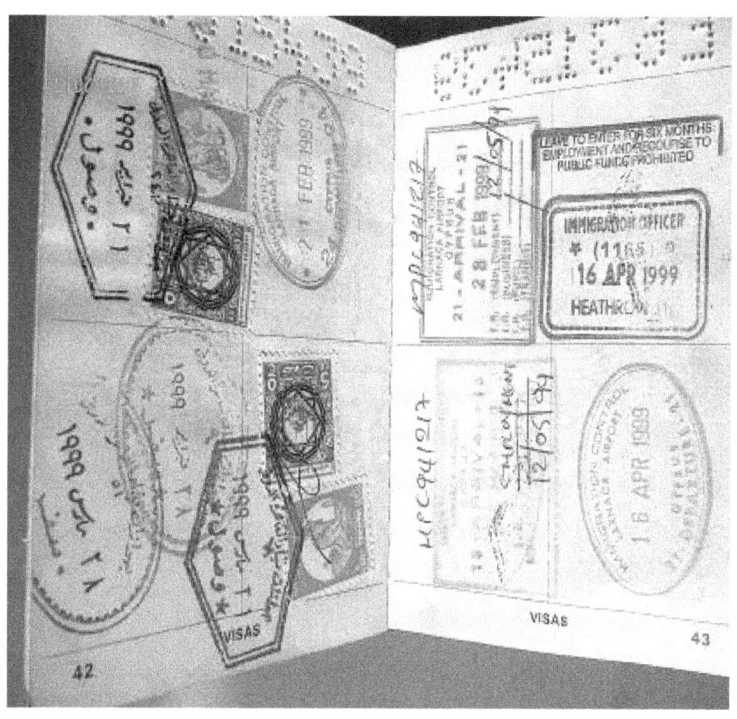

Egypt
& India

Chapter One

Surprise Encounter
Egypt (2002)

We turn the corner. A car coming towards us suddenly stops. With a screech of brakes it immediately reverses, speeding up road 315, taking off over the speed bumps. Four wheels in the air!

'What's happening?' cries Jan, grabbing my arm.

'It's my old landlord, Sabry. I haven't seen him for ages. One look at me, and he's taken off. Backwards!'

'What's his problem?'

'I don't really know. It's a long story, Jan. I'm still trying to make sense of it.'

Back in the flat in Sharia 306 I start recalling that time, in mid 1999, when I went to live in Sabry's block of flats.

****

Flat Hunting
Egypt (1999)

I remember walking down the tree-lined streets of the garden suburb of Maadi in greater Cairo. Lars Ericson, a work colleague, was helping me look for a flat. Flame trees with giant red blooms, the stripy pinks of the Chinese Orchid trees, and the blazing boughs of the bright yellow Cassia alongside the deep purple of the Jacarandas graced the streets. In the 1800s, the British laid out Maadi when they put in the railway. I've seen the same sort of area in New Delhi—a colourful inheritance for people: lovely Victorian mansions in large gardens, sweeping lawns and most of all, beautiful flowering trees, rarely seen elsewhere in both cities.

Most of the graceful homes have made way for economically viable ugly apartment blocks. Murky monochrome; each high-rise defaced by dirt and sand. Each building boasting precarious balconies and rows of air conditioners cleaving to the walls like barnacles to boats. Snakes of electrical wiring coiled together towards the rooftops; illegal connections to outbreaks of mushroom satellite dishes.

I needed accommodation because I was finally moving to Egypt after five years on Cyprus and travelling to Egypt three or four times a year. Now a friend from Adelaide was taking over my job and I would be free to live in this huge city and work with the editorial team of a much-loved Arabic youth magazine.

As a single foreign female, there were certain criteria to be considered. For security reasons, the flat couldn't be on the ground floor open to the street. The first or second floor was preferred. The building itself had to be secured by a locked gate leading into a front garden or a locked front door with a *Bowab* - the door keeper - in attendance. The flat had to be of moderate tariff as my allowance was small and landlords tended to expect expatriates to be rich. If I were the only single foreign female in the area I would be a source of continual gossip and surveillance. To reduce that would be an advantage.

One time we found ourselves in a street ankle deep in sand and rubbish. I was puzzled by car tyres cut in half leading from the street up to the building we were entering. Lars muttered something about a drainage system. Inside, the apartment looked like it hadn't been lived in for millennia. Heavy grey brown dust covered everything and the mattress made me gag. The dirty olive-green tiles in the kitchen, viewed from the front door, reminded me of a grotty corner pub in the back streets of Sydney.

Raylene Pearce

We viewed several unsuitable lodgings, always asking, 'Is this an appropriate place for a single foreign female to dwell?' In a city where it is never appropriate for a single woman to live alone whatever her race, this was a big ask. As Personnel Director I had to consider whether my flat was suitable for other single women to visit anytime, day or night.

Having streetlights would help, and easy access to a main road with taxis cruising by every two minutes would also be a plus. My colleagues were an eclectic mix of Egyptians, Koreans, Norwegians, Aussies, New Zealanders, Americans, English, Irish and Scots, Welsh and Swedes, Canadians, Dutch and Germans, and many of them were single females.

All day Lars and I trudged the labyrinthine passages. A good thing were the throngs of people shopping and gossiping, filling the streets. Donkeys braying and car horns competing with each other filled the air. It was a hot July day and we were about to give up.

Would there ever be a suitable place for me in this huge city?

****

Disappointed, we arrived at an apartment several streets away where, some months before, I had spoken about a flat with the landlord, Sabry. His asking price was too high and so was the flat—on the fifth floor! My bones could not have coped with the climb.

There was a lift, but it didn't work. Actually, it wasn't really there, just the promise of one: the door, the buttons, and nothing else. It gave the appearance of a sort of luxury along with the shiny pink marble walls, but that's all it was, a façade. I did not know then that the word 'façade' was to be appropriate in the future.

There was a locked front door opening into the pink foyer, but there was no way of opening the door other than making the journey downstairs and manually opening it. There was an intercom at the gate that allowed you to know who was standing there, which was invaluable.

Night Journeys

My experiences in other Middle Eastern abodes taught me that having a fifth floor apartment makes you either extremely fit or, in my case at my age, completed pooped.

During the previous visit, Sabry showed me an apartment on the first floor. It was a replica of the fifth floor flat he was offering me. This flat on the first floor had been used to store equipment when the block was painted. The linoleum floor, the colour of silage, was randomly splattered with blobs of sickly porridge, the cream paint spewed on the linoleum.

I remember saying to Sabry, 'I wouldn't live here with that awful floor.'

So this time, I swallowed my pride, 'Sabry, I have looked everywhere for a flat, but found nothing suitable. Nothing convenient. Nothing. Have you got any ideas?'

He then surprised me by saying, 'I want you to live here. Come and see what I am offering.'

He then brought the price down and offered me—yes, you guessed it—the flat with the awful floors. Me, and my big mouth! Needless to say, I accepted his offer.

Regarding the awful floor, one friend at home suggested that each time I entered my new home I should look up. That's an idea! Looking up meant that you looked straight into the jungle of dodgy electrical wiring coiled up around light fittings and sticking out of walls. There was a distinct feeling that came with this upward looking: fear—fear of fire and fear of electrocution.

Looking out wasn't much of an option either. The view was depressing. The next-door apartment's dung-coloured cement wall with the ubiquitous coils of electrical cables and noisy air conditioners greeted my disenchanted gaze. A front window onto the street had a better view with a flame tree making a statement of beauty when in full burst of red.

The lack of view was only outweighed by the wind tunnel funnelling twenty-four hour noise from the *Midan el Arab* in the next street. This huge roundabout, resembling a giant octopus, was used by about a million people daily as they travelled along the five converging streets, the railway line, the path to the mosque and the main *souk* - the market. A cacophony of noise pulsated within spitting distance of my new bedroom. I was wrong about the twenty-four hour traffic noise. Between the hour of three o'clock in the morning and four, before the first call to prayer, it was quiet. One whole hour!

During the day the *Midan el Arab* and the adjacent *souk* offered much interest. It was there I practiced my Arabic as I bought my apples, mangoes in season (like nothing else on earth as delicious) various vegetables mostly grown in the delta to the north where the Nile emptied into the Mediterranean. A goods train came through twice a day. At the sound of an elephant's bellow there was a mad scramble as the people who set up their stalls on top of the railway line scrambled to safety. As soon as the train passed through, back on the tracks they'd go.

Across the railway line was a small building where a long trail of women lined up every day to get the government sponsored *eesh baladi* (whole-meal pita bread). It's very cheap, nourishing, and delicious too. I lined up one day, but was embarrassed when I became the centre of interest. I got the distinct impression that the women didn't approve of me, a 'rich' expat taking advantage of the government's initiative to distribute cheap bread to its poor. So I never went again. But sometimes, Egyptian friends would bring me a plastic bag full, knowing how much I liked it.

****

So why did I take the flat? The people across the landing from the first floor flat were friends and it was in walking distance from the office.

Before long I had the flat looking really nice. Taking advantage of the local *souk*, I bought Bedouin rugs for the floor and the *Khan el Khalil* (the great bazaar) downtown Cairo offered many throws, recycled blue glass, and knickknacks to make my flat an attractive place.

Night Journeys

Soon more associates from other aid and development groups arrived, introduced by us to our obliging landlord. For twelve months we were a happy, friendly international family. I spent a great deal of time, sharing hospitality with the expats in the building and Egyptian friends and visitors from many lands.

No one was ever bothered by the floors.

I had no presentiment that I should have looked more closely at my gift.

****

'For I know the plans I have for you,' says the LORD,
'plans to prosper you and not to harm you,
plans to give you hope and a future.'

Jeremiah 20:11

The flat I first lived in until Sept 11th 2001

Chapter Two

The Girl on a Night Journey
India (1991)

We sat gazing out over the valley, the seven layers of the lower Himalayas spread out before us. Each step into the beauty of this spot literally took my breath away. While my new friend walked with a graceful lope, I struggled, as each step upwards challenged my lungs. Felicity was young, tall and lovely, her long golden hair sometimes twisted up, but today it flowed loose and gleaming in the winter sunshine. Her red beanie covered her ears, the red offsetting the blue of her parka and the colourful striped Nepali scarf. Both of us were well rugged up as it was January, and being in northern India we were further north than Kathmandu.

Felicity was from England and I from another flattish country down under.

'I never knew it could be so beautiful,'

'Neither did I,' I said.

We sat in companionable silence. We had been taking short walks most days. I had trained hard, walking up and down the gentle Adelaide hills before I took off for the Indian subcontinent. But at 2100 metres, the air was such that one step left me gasping for air and void of energy. And they called this the foothills!

I had been staying with colleagues at Woodstock School in North India. This young woman was also staying with them. In her backpack was a notebook with names in it. She was wandering from place to place and sometimes stayed with people listed in her little book. A colleague in England had given her names for the Indian leg of her solitary journey.

Felicity and I talked. I don't know what about, but she sought my company, so between gasps for breath, I guess I had opportunity to listen. She was a very troubled young woman, in her gap year before going to university. After North India, she planned to go to Varanasi to stay in a convent.

Months before, Felicity had been involved in a horrific car crash which took the life of her mother. This journey she was on was the way she was trying to cope with the loss and the grief. There was another lost-ness too — she had lost herself spiritually. In the months leading up to the crash, she had become rebellious and had fought with her mother. This had lead to massive feelings of guilt, and unknown to both of us, this time together was a prelude to her regaining her faith and trust in God.

I remember putting her on the enormously long, noisy, packed train going south. The carriages had three layers of bunks along the sides with a narrow passageway between. I was travelling with Jillian Anderson at the time, and we positioned the frail girl in one of the top bunks, into a corner of the carriage against a wall. Her backpack and supplies from the shop at Dehra Dun station were piled around her like a fort. Balancing on the bottom bunk, we lent over her and prayed for her. We asked God's protection for the train journey. We asked that she would find the convent with ease, which was asking a lot in this complex, immensely populated country.

Felicity said she was grateful for our encouragement. Another list of names was added to her notebook. Then the train moved off into the night, taking its huge consignment of human beings with it.

With the adventures on four continents that lay ahead of me, Felicity all but faded from my mind.

****

Part Two

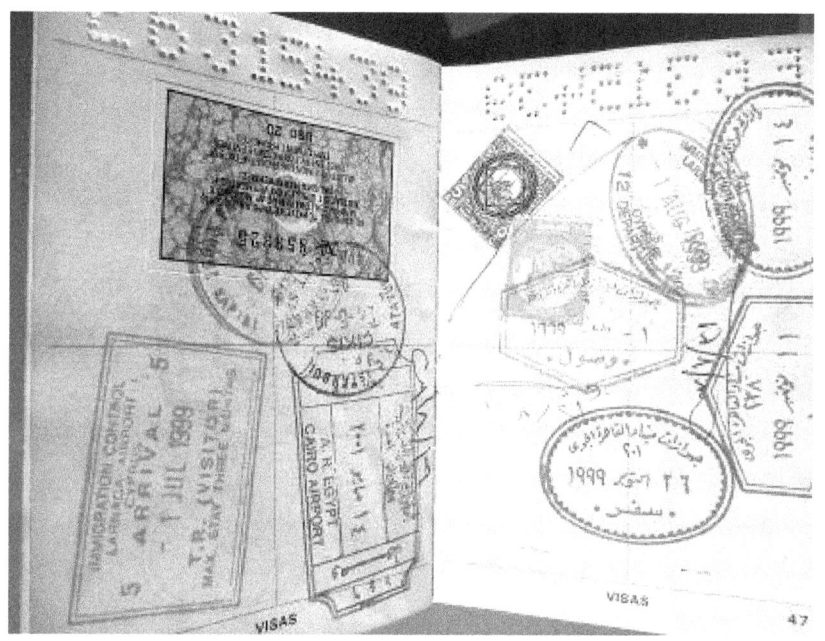

South Australia

Chapter Three

Growing Character

How did I come to this place anyway? Why was I about to move into an apartment block in Cairo that was to later prove to be a mysterious and possibly dangerous situation?

I might need to go back a long way to my childhood to partially explain.

****

Drain Danger
(1954)

I was an adventurous child and as the older sister very bossy. I gave my brother David, who was three years younger, a hard time. Once I hung him on the clothesline, the type you prop up. I propped it up and the silly boy let go! I raced off down the back lane while he, with his face pouring blood, screamed for Mum. But there were other times when he got back at me. My character needed reforming.

When I was ten I got stuck in a drain. My gang was made up of three boys aged eight, ten, and eleven. We were playing in the main open cement drain that ran through the suburb of Unley.

David was there too because Mum had insisted that his big sister look after him. I thought he was too much of a sook to be in my gang, but he trotted along with us. There was Brian who was in my class and Mike and Paul whose father owned the corner shop

Night Journeys

where we got paper funnels of lollies once a week. Sometimes their mum put an extra musk stick or chocolate bullet in our funnels for a surprise.

We had been told not to play in the drain. It slunk behind the local hotel and we had all been regaled with terrible tales of dreadful drunk men who might grab us and take us away and we would never be seen again.

This particular day I led my gang further along the drain to where a huge circular drainpipe emptied into the large cement open drain we used as our adventure playground. I decided to find out where the drainpipe led to, so the boys hoisted me up onto the ledge of the tunnel.

I started off on my hands and knees, and soon I had to wriggle along on my stomach. Ahead, I could see some dim light but as the light in the tunnel decreased, so the diameter of the pipe decreased as well. Soon I felt my shoulders being pressed against the walls but I pushed on confident that the light at the end of the tunnel meant the end of my journey. Yes it was the end of my journey, but the pipe ended in a narrow rectangular opening into the gutter of the street above. Now I was in trouble.

There was no sign of the boys, so I start to yell.

'Help!' My mouth pressed up against the storm-water pipe opening.

All of a sudden David peered down at me.

'Don't just stand there,' I screamed, 'Help me.'

'How?' said David, 'You won't fit through this'. He kicked the gutter and sent dirt into my face.

Mike's shoes appeared, then his knees as he crouched down, 'It's late. Mum'll have tea on the table. Gotta go.'

'Don't leave me here!' I screamed, infuriated that they would leave me like this just because it was time for tea! So the boys went off leaving little David squatting in the gutter, his hands under his chin, his elbows on his knees.

'You'll have to go back, Raylene.'

'I can't turn, I'm stuck.'

'Don't turn, just push your way back, or I'll have to get Mum and then you'll be in big trouble.'

'Don't go David, don't tell Mum, I'll give you my next lot of lollies if you don't tell.'

'O.K.' said David, feeling his power.

Bit by bit I puffed and pushed my way back down the drain. To start with it was hard going and the light had faded from the gutter opening and the gloom was scary. But soon the tunnel widened and with bruised elbows and scraped knees, my jumper torn and shoes scuffed, I slid with a thump back into the now dark and deserted open drain. I landed heavily with no gang to assist me.

I vowed that I would get even with those boys who left me in the tunnel where I could have died, just because their dinner was ready.

Here is Millie, my granddaughter, then aged four, taking in the location of this segment of my memoir. The pavement is different but the place was the same when I came to the dead end of the drain. (2007)

****

Night Journeys

The Red Tartan Skirt

Outside our house in Marion Street, Unley is a sign "Sturt Supporters Only".

We always check that whoever takes that prized position, near Cambridge Terrace that runs into the Unley Oval, supports the right team.

I'm talking about Aussie Rules Football and the year this happened was 1954. Our team was the Double Blues, the famous Sturt Football Club.

My home in Marion St. Unley as it looked in 2007.

The gang assembles. I'm still cross with them for deserting me in my hour of need and for putting me in little David's power. I hand out the hessian bags and we make our way to the hallowed ground where we pick up bottles and call out 'Come on Sturts' at the top of our lungs.

Raylene Pearce

On this notorious day I have the bright idea of going out the Members Stand Gate by the grandstand as if we had paid to come in.

So after the match ends, we make our way to the opposite end of our usual working area. This is a grassy knoll where the grown-ups stand and yell abuse at the umpire and cheer whenever Sturt kicks a goal. By the time our little legs get around to the Members Stand Gate, it's closed! We look up at its grand façade, sigh deeply, and turn around and proceed to our usual entrance, which looks very small and very far away.

'OK, we cut across the ground,' I call, as I start to climb over the small picket fence that surrounds the playing field.

I'll never forget that day.

The Grandstand 2007 at the Sturt Football Oval,
No member's gate or picket fence. Sturts still play here. In 2015 a picket fence was erected and the oval re-named the Peter Motley Oval. 'Come on Sturts!'

Night Journeys

We get to the middle of the oval and see in the distance that the giant gate the ordinary people go through – our entrance – is closed too, and there doesn't seem to be anyone around. We must have dawdled collecting the last lot of bottles on our way to the Members Stand Gate. Now everyone has gone home!

'Right,' I say, my arms folded across my chest, my feet apart in my leader position.

'Sturts play here in two weeks' time. So by the time they open the gates we will have starved to death and the crows will have picked out our eyes.'

That did it. David starts to cry. 'I don't want to die. I don't want crows eating out my eyes. I want my Mum. I want my dinner.'

Boys are always thinking of their stomachs!

'Oright. I have a plan.'

Standing before the huge tin gate, with the three rows of barbed wire flayed out on top, I declare to the gang that I will rescue them.

'I'll climb out of here and get the police.'

So up I go, my tartan skirt swinging in the breeze. I remember lying across the barbed wire leaning out over the footpath and my jumper snagging on all the barbs. I took ages to free myself and, dangling by the final strand, I let myself free fall the seven or eight feet to the ground, opening the graze on my just healed knees from the previous episode in the drain.

On all fours I begin to lift my head. My eyes catch sight of a row of scuffed black lace-up shoes on the ground in front of me. As my chin continues to lift I see four pairs of grey socks bunching, sprouting four pairs of bare legs revealing David, Mike, Paul and Brian grinning their heads off.

'We found a hole in the hedge,' says David.

Mortified, I grab him, holding his arms tight, 'Don't you breathe anything about this to Mum, or you will be sorry for the rest of your life! And don't you say anything about my skirt.'

Raylene Pearce

We look up.
Half a red tartan skirt flaps away on the barbed wire.

****

Later, as Mum places the dinner on the table, she asks David why his big sister isn't there.

'Oh she's coming,' nods the co-conspirator relishing another dose of power.

I'm busy digging a hole at the back of the wood shed and burying my skirt.

Some weeks later Mum, in a puzzled way says, 'Y'know, I can't seem to find your red tartan skirt anywhere. Where on earth can it be?' She stresses the word 'earth'.

I guess it is a rhetorical question, as my deceased red tartan skirt is very much a part of the earth by now. My shoulders indicate that it is as much a mystery to me as to her.

I regret to say that as close as I was to my mother, I never actually told her about what really happened to my red tartan skirt.

There never was a replacement.

But David and I never forgot how we had scared the daylights out of ourselves when we thought we would die and have our eyes pecked out by crows when we were locked in the Unley Oval.

I often wonder what the Sturt footballers thought of my tartan flag blowing in the wind atop the old iron gate of the Sturt Football Club when they next came to play a home match.

And I can't remember us ever going bottle collecting there again.

****

Night Journeys

At the end of my tenth year of life, the family moves to our new house in Balmoral Ave, Brighton.

The vineyard at the end of our street, from whence great shotgun blasts of noise erupt at regular intervals to scare away the birds, becomes our grape picking (stealing) adventure playground. I make a cubby down the back yard having found a large cache of gold (pyrites) and another gang evolves.

This time our adversary is whoever it is shooting the birds. Next time it could be us!

While back in the old house in Unley, behind the woodshed in its lonely grave, the remains of my red tartan skirt lay buried.

****

> Remember not the sins of my youth and my rebellious ways;
> according to your love remember me,
> for you are good, O LORD.
>
> Psalm 25 v 7

Chapter Four

Into Bed with Nanna
Henley Beach (1952)

My life during these years was blessed by two women; my Nanna and her daughter, my Mother. I want them in this book because without their influence, I would never have developed the character needed to live the life I led.

*****

So many times we had been in bed together, Nanna and I.

My first memories, beginning when I was two years old, revolved around the big house at Henley Beach where Nanna and Grandpa lived. Right on the esplanade this wonderful house stood. It had 18 rooms and a garage for Grandpa's *Vauxhall* and a workroom where Grandpa, a strong, short man in his fifties, with farming in his blood, repaired all our broken toys.

There was a long passageway leading from the huge living room at the back to a sunroom opening to the sea. At night my cousins and I would frighten each other, screeching as we ran up the passage in the dark. The main bedroom had an exquisitely cut glass door, which played a prominent role in our night games as we made grotesque faces with the light of a torch through the prisms. My bed was a small mattress with blankets and snowy white sheets made up on the floor, between the beautiful cut-glass door and dark oak wardrobe.

I was snug and secure. I remember the big mantelpiece too, made of marble with a tiny bottle of eucalyptus oil placed at one end, reputed to cure every ill. Beside the bottle of eucalyptus was a fine sculpture of a beautiful lady holding a seagull. She was a creamy colour and Nanna, who was short, slightly built but strong, just like her daughter, my mother, would lift me up and let me stroke the bird's neck.

Each morning Grandpa would sit on his side of the bed and throw his pyjamas at me. Then, as he went off to get breakfast and the newspaper, I would climb into bed with Nanna. We would cuddle up giggling till our breakfast came. Grandpa would arrive with a tray and two steaming bowls of porridge and a cup of tea for Nanna. There would always be a fresh flower placed on the tray. What spoilt females we were! Then, while I got ready for my day on the beach, Nanna and Grandpa did the crossword puzzle in *The Advertiser*.

The evenings were best. After we had done the dishes Nanna and I would feed the greedy, squawky seagulls from the red steps in front of the house; Nanna calling 'Gully, gully, gully' as they honed in for their nightly nibbles. Then we would go for a stroll along the beach watching the red golden lights in the sky.

She's probably about four. Arms and legs crossed, mouth open, sitting on the red steps at Nanna and Grandpa's house on the esplanade at Henley Beach.

Raylene Pearce

During the summer when the sideshows filled the Square we would watch the beauty pageant and listen to the big bands. After that I would have a ride on the merry-go-round. Later, we would walk back chomping on toffee apples or fairy floss and tell grandpa all the news.

One night I will never forget. In the middle of the beauty pageant everything stopped, and the Mayor came to the microphone. He read out a statement telling us that our beloved King had died peacefully in his sleep. Far away in England a middle-aged man died and it affected ordinary people at a summer fair at Henley Beach, South Australia. I remember a hush, then a moan that welled up from the crowd gathered before the bandstand. For all the days of my life, King George VI had been my King and now he was dead.

I had made scrapbooks of pictures of the Royal Family from the *Australian Women's Weekly* and now my grief blocked out the fact that the beautiful Princess Elizabeth would now become our Queen. All I could do was cry. I remember the comforting arms of my Nanna as we made our way among the sombre crowd, all festivities cancelled, towards the great house on the Esplanade.

Grandpa had already heard on the radio of the King's death, so he was waiting for us at the top of the red stairs leading to the glass door of the sunroom with two mugs of cocoa ready to comfort us.

On the evenings when we didn't go to the fair, we did the next best thing. Leaving Grandpa to his account books at the great oval table that filled the huge bay window in the living room, Nanna and I would get ready for bed. Then we would turn out the lights and snuggle up in expectation of the wonders that would flow out of the soft golden glow of the mantel radio.

What wonderful treats would be in store tonight? The opening bars of *Night Beat* would send shivers up my spine as *Randy Stone*, cub reporter, would investigate a lead on a new story. Or we would worry and chew our nails about the lost people in *Missing Persons' Bureau*, or get all excited as *Inspector West* found another clue and brought the criminal to justice. *Harry Dearth's Playhouse* was a great favourite and grandpa would bring us a mug of hot chocolate when he heard the famous signature tune indicating the finish of the latest drama.

Sometimes Nanna would read me a favourite storybook, *Lassie Come Home*, *Blinky Bill* or *The Gum-nut Babies*. Other times she would make up a story on the spot, which always included the adventures of her first-born grandchild. I loved her reading the stories from the Bible and we would raid the dress-up box for costumes to act out the stories.

****

That which was from the beginning,
which we have heard,
which we have seen with our eyes,
which we have looked at and
our hands have touched –
this we proclaim concerning the Word of Life.
The life appeared; we have seen it and testify to it,
and we proclaim to you the eternal life,
which was with the Father and has appeared to us.
We proclaim to you what we have seen and heard,
so that you also may have fellowship with us.
And our fellowship is with the Father
and with his Son, Jesus Christ.
We write this to make our joy complete.

John, the disciple of Christ, first letter v 1-4

Chapter Five

Direction at Last
(1959 – 1962)

When I was fourteen I was attending the Hamilton Park Methodist Church, that very important year when I publicly gave my life to Jesus at the Billy Graham Crusade.

I was at a girl's camp at Nunyara in the Adelaide Hills. Someone came and got me and took me home. My father was ill again with war neurosis. He was in our next-door neighbour's garden fighting the Japanese in his pyjamas. Dad was reliving the horror of a certain night. He'd been calling for his little baby and his wife. I was horrified and as a fourteen year old I was filled with shame. Mum had called our minister.

John Rees came and crouched down in the garden with Dad. This is what he said: 'Ray, you do not have to carry the guilt of that time.'

(The time he was speaking of was when Dad was in Borneo in the last year of the war. His platoon mistakenly shot up their own men. A section of the platoon had been sent up the hill to check out the enemy. Later, those soldiers were sent stumbling down the hill by the Japanese with hands tied behind their backs, their mouths gagged. Dad's section heard them coming. They called out and there was no reply. So they opened fire. In the morning of that evil night, Dad's section moved to the base of the hill and looked down into the dead eyes of their mates.)

Then John Rees said. 'On the cross Jesus took into himself all the sin of the world. All the grief, the sorrow, the wars, the peace, the guilt, the suffering, the mistakes and the atrocities done to man by man. He took it and defeated the power of all those things, so that you may never need to carry that guilt any more.'

From that night onwards my dad grew in the assurance of that truth and was no more troubled by the horrific images of that dreadful night in Borneo. Instead of shame, I was filled with pride as my father, living out his freedom in Christ, went into youth ministry at our church and local preaching.

I remember, between the age of 16 and 18, before I went nursing, I used to go with Dad as he preached in little churches in the Adelaide hills. I would read the Scriptures and sometimes tell a children's story. Dad's favourite Bible character was Simon Peter, the fisherman, a disciple of Jesus. This was great training for me for when I grew up.

****

The Bloody Slides
Adelaide

Mrs Saunders dragged her chair into the living room from the passageway. The others shuffled closer to the black-and-white flickering screen in the corner to make room for the late arrival. The neighbours had assembled and I was being tumbled off to bed in a bad mood because *Medic* was about to start.

'Raylene, you are too young to watch this. Off to bed and no arguing.'

That was Dad, who thought it too 'adult' for me. Black-and-white blood and guts; how could that cause me any harm?

I was going to be a nurse in four years' time anyway.

I already knew what I was going to be when I grew up. I knew that my nursing would not take place among the fat people of Australia, but the skinny people of India. Miss Nicholls, my grade-seven teacher, was from Kerala in South India and I was enamoured of her country and the stories she told us.

I had a plan. In first year High I was asked what I wanted to be when I grew up.

I said, 'Missionary Nurse'.

The teacher put down just 'nurse'.

'No,' I said. 'Missionary Nurse. I'm going to nurse the poor people of India.'

And here I was, fourteen years old and sent to bed while the neighbours who would never bandage a bloodied arm or pass a scalpel to a handsome doctor were watching my programme.

I did watch it once, so I was an expert on its content. Dad had a meeting after church and Mum had said, 'I'll let you watch this just once, but don't tell your father'.

This was a surprise because Mum usually said, 'Wait till your father gets home and I'll tell him what you did'.

She also knew that I had already read all the books in my parents' bookcase beside the fireplace, including Morton Thompson's *Not as a Stranger*. It was all about doctors and nurses. In it, a little boy cuts off his penis. His mum had said, 'If you keep playing with that, I'll cut it off'. So he did it for her.

I considered this gory information, taken into my fourteen-year-old consciousness, a very grown-up thing to experience. The people coming to our home, as the first house in Balmoral Ave to get television, would never see such a thing in *Medic*.

****

Then one Saturday night a missionary doctor who was working in India, of all places, came to our church. He unpacked his bag and brought out his slides. I will never forget those giant technicolour images. No puny black-and-white pictures from the *Kreisler* in the corner of our lounge room. Here the blood was bright red and the gowns and masks gleaming white. The huge ovarian cyst held in the surgeon's cupped hands was the size of a fully-grown watermelon, striped pink, blue, and red. And the glint in the eyes of the doctor shone into the camera, his trophy held out for all to see.

This girl drank it all in. This was to be my world.

After the doctor packed up his bag, I followed him across the tiny square of lawn in front of the church hall. I stood close while he opened the car door to put in his bag and slide projector. He turned and saw a skinny, long-legged, fourteen-year-old girl with short, dark-brown hair and a straight fringe, going through her 'really ugly' stage of development, gawking at him.

He smiled and gave me the courage to blurt, 'Can I come to India with you, Dr Pike?'

He was so kind. I remember him asking me what I wanted to be when I grew up. I had my answer ready.

Then he said, 'When you complete your nursing training you must keep in touch with the Methodist Overseas Missions.' (MOM)

I nodded. Mum was the president of the *Methodist Overseas Missionary Fellowship Ladies Auxiliary* at church. She would know what to do.

Then he said, 'I'll be delighted to have you join us in northern India as soon as your training is complete.'

I have never forgotten that moment – I now had a goal!

****

I had kept my goal alive all through the years of High School.

My Heavenly Father set up people to help me keep the goal alive throughout a two-year involvement in the grown-up world of office work. I was the Assistant Organiser for the *Kate Cocks' Memorial Babies Home* in the office at 33 Pirie St, Adelaide. Deaconess Phyllis Bonython was my boss.

She was pivotal during those two years in keeping me on track and opening me to God's grace. She joined my Mother and Nanna in teaching me through the example of compassion for people in great need and how to love the unlovely.

On the ground floor of 33 Pirie Street was the *Methodist Overseas Missions* (*MOM* office), with the Rev Roger Brown in charge. He helped to keep me on track too.

Sometimes keeping on track involved a few twists and turns. Sometimes I went round in circles. I was not aware that my Heavenly Father was re-shaping me. He had a plan, so that I could be used by him for His Glory, and a blessing to others.

****

Trust in the LORD with all your heart
and lean not on your own understanding;
in all your ways acknowledge him,
and he will make your paths straight.

Proverbs 3 v 5 & 6

Chapter Six

Memorial Memories
I Remember You
North Adelaide (1966)

A room of my own! A room with a view!

Long before Virginia Woolf or EM Forster entered my consciousness and bookshelf, I had a room of my own with a view. I was in charge of my first ward in the Memorial Hospital with a view over the Adelaide parklands. I had five men, all squeaky-clean, well starched, and ready for breakfast in their snowy-white beds. What joy!

In 1966 I was in my third year of nursing. I turned to survey my domain. Four gleaming patients tightly laced into their spotless white beds, their inner sheets pleated to allow toes a place to frolic. Under each armpit, a draw sheet neatly placed over their snowy-white quilts prevented the ubiquitous newspaper print impacting on a perfect bed. Bed tables in place, taste buds at the ready—ready for breakfast.

Only Mr Bennett couldn't sit up with such anticipation. Once the breakfast was delivered I would sit down beside him. As I fed him I would quietly chat about this and that. Mr Rossetti, my southern Italian, had a robust appetite but tended to move his porridge around without much enthusiasm. I had my suspicions about his food supply. I was in the habit of sneaking in his extensive family to see him each afternoon and evening. In those days there were strict instructions that limited visitors per patient. This noisy mob came laden with mysterious packages. With my *'buongiorno'* and a smattering of other English-Italian phrases learned from being in the chorus of *The Gondo-*

liers at Brighton High School, I was a great favourite with his visitors. They reckoned I was 'one of the family'. It appeared that I looked just like cousin Rosa Maria.

One afternoon I bowed out of my room with a Gilbert-and-Sullivan flourish, smack bang into the ample bosom of Matron, who was making an unexpected visit. She was investigating the undignified noise emanating from my room, a few doors from her sacred precinct. I'd had a few run-ins with matron over the years, but lately we had to collaborate for me to have a particular day off.

Mr Yani, a robust Hungarian, was being discharged. He had declared he was taking me with him. One day he aggressively pronounced his love for me. He jammed me between the stove and the sink in the nurses' kitchen. Matron was most sympathetic to my plight and Mr Yani slunk off home with his hernia healed and his nurse out of reach.

Mr Bennett had been in with us for several weeks. He was suffering from an inoperable brain tumour. Each day I would give him a sponge bath, rub his back with methylated spirits and check and massage his pressure points while quietly talking to him. I never heard his voice. I would gently comb his hair and place him on his side to await his wife's visits. His corner of the room was the quiet spot. I don't think he was even aware of my endless vocal interactions with Mr Yani, or of Mr Rossetti and all his relatives.

I was one of those cheery nurses. I always made a fun time out of injections and manual excavations of impacted faeces. That was one of the administrations of mercy that I remember for a man in bed two. What a dear old man, what an embarrassed man, what an uncomfortable man. But I unblocked him and what a cheer went up among my men when the results became obvious to all!

But Mr Bennett remained silent, his sky-blue eyes sometimes watching, mostly closed. Then one morning I was standing at the end of his snowy-white bed. I was wondering if there was anything else I could do to make him more comfortable. This was something drilled into us at the Memorial. The patient was the most important person.

Night Journeys

Their comfort and care was supreme. Nurses' needs came way down the ladder and we never questioned it. Why should it be any other way? But as an adult patient many years later I discovered that this was no longer always the case. Anyway, in the olden days the patients came first. You would never leave their room or bedside without that final check to see if something else could be done for them.

My final check of Mr Bennett extended to a long look—a look of recognition—a returning to a precious memory. But how could it be? How could this man, my patient for four weeks, someone of whom I had almost daily care, someone with whom I had talked through all his procedures—how could I not recognise him? He was changed. His tumour had done its work. It was eight years since he had taught me in grade six; the only male teacher I had for my primary education. And I loved him! I remember crying my heart out when I moved into grade seven. I couldn't have him for my teacher anymore.

Now I walked towards his head. He was resting on his right cheek and I crouched down beside him, my face inches from his.

I said, 'Mr Bennett do you remember me? Raylene Greenslade, grade six, Paringa Park Primary School?'

Mr Bennett stirred; his blue eyes looked straight into mine. With a slight smile he spoke: the only words I would ever hear him say.

'Yes, I remember you. You used to talk all the time.'

What's changed?

****

Raylene Pearce

Night Rescue

'How about going into town for an ice-cream?' I ask Robin Osborne as we come off duty at eight pm. Robin and I started training together in 1963 and remained friends all through our time at Memorial and after.

We leave the hospital, walk the twenty minutes into the city, buy the gelato, and return along the well-lit road. As we pass the Torrens Parade Ground, the Army Reserve is completing their parade drill. We cross the bridge over the river and two soldiers come alongside us. One of them grabs me and drags me through the red–and-yellow cannas in the gardens between the footpath and the river, my legs bleeding from the scratches.

Robin stands with the second soldier guarding her on the footpath, screaming, 'Don't go in the bushes!'

I have no choice. I am pushed up against the trunk of a tall gum tree just in front of one of the rowing sheds. It happens so quickly.

I look into the young man's contorted face and drawing on my nursing instincts, start to gently talk to him.

'Stop, or you'll be sorry. You'll get into such trouble. There are witnesses.'

'I don't care,' he snarls. 'It was hell tonight and I just want to hurt someone.'

By now he has my arms spread out back around the trunk of the tree as he presses into me. I keep calm.

'You'll be in big trouble. Don't you care about yourself?' I whisper against his ear, appealing to his own survival instincts.

Suddenly, I am on the other side of the tree! I'm free!

I fly across Sir Edwin Smith Avenue, the Adelaide Oval on my left.

Robin, taking courage, flees after me, our feet scarcely touching the ground. We race alongside the Cross of Sacrifice Memorial Garden and enter the hospital grounds through a side gate on Pennington Terrace. We race up the stairs of the nurses' home, turn into the tiny kitchen on the first floor and perch on the bench. We sit there shaking as the delayed shock takes hold of us.

'I'm still trying to take it in,' I say, sipping sweetened tea, the shakes beginning to subside. 'One minute I'm pinned against the tree and the next I've slipped out of his reach and taken off like a shot. It was like I was flying.'

'It must have been your guardian angel,' Robin says.

'That has to be it. I still can't get over how calm I was, and able to speak to him and how I actually cared about what might happen to him!'

****

When I was in my third year of nursing training at the Memorial hospital I heard that Dr Pike, and a whole lot of other missionaries were refused visas and had to leave India. That sort of skewed my goal.

****

"You have heard that it was said,
'love your neighbour and hate your enemy.'
But I tell you: Love your enemies
and pray for those who persecute you,
that you may be sons and daughters of your Father in Heaven.

Matthew 5 v 43

Chapter Seven

Night of Storms
Northern Territory (1968)

After I completed my nursing training I married and went to work on *The Island* in Northern Australia. Prior to that, Peter had been called up in the first National Service intake during the Vietnam War. Our courtship was mainly separation and letter writing. He completed his two years posting at Ingleburn in NSW as a Training Officer. We took off north and entered an entirely new culture. The Methodist Overseas Mission in Darwin arranged for us to work on *The Island* as volunteers. Peter worked in the gardens, and I was the third nursing sister in the hospital.

Because of the sensitivity of Yulgnu culture I am giving western names to the people in this night journey.

****

I ease open the louvre windows. Spears of rain pierce my eyes. I quickly close the slats. It's nine o'clock in the evening and I'm due at the hospital at ten. I grab a torch and some toilet paper and zigzag through the mango madness, dodging the swooping bats. I hate those bats. Bowed low, I burst into the wonky outhouse that hugs the corner of the backyard. Inside I let the light settle on the tightly packed red-and-black beetles pulsating on the ceiling. I hate those beetles. Lifting the lid I check for red-back spiders and snakes and do not tarry. I'll not make any further comment as to my opinion of these latter two.

Night Journeys

The tiny room does not invite quiet contemplation. The major side effect of such a place is constipation!

I fight my way back through the rain and the bats. I check on my husband. He is asleep under the mosquito net. I have a momentary shock as a passing car lights up the room. His tanned body takes on the aspect of a stranger. My first thought is, 'Where is he? What have they done with him? A stupid thought. I don't need to be spooked on a night like this.'

Our living quarter on *The Island* is tiny. Twelve paces by ten on the outside. The walls made of planks and built under the mission house and beside the carport. The bedroom is the same size as the double bed. To get in and out, we have to climb over the end of the bed, the bed-head up against the louver windows. I back into the minute living room and make a cup of tea, thinking about Wendy who hadn't turned up to clinic today.

The night before, she stood at my door, calling out and howling that her baby was dead. It was late and I had to crawl out from the tangle of mosquito netting, fumble for the torch, and meet the small group of *yolgnu* huddling beside the door. Wendy handed me the baby, his eyes glued shut with thick globs of pus. I scraped the tiny eyelashes free of their prison with my fingernails and spat in both eyes, wiping them with my hanky. (I did it that way to demonstrate that she could do it herself.) The baby's eyes struggled to open.

'He's alive!' His family rejoice.

I tell her to bring him to clinic the next day where I would put good medicine in his eyes. But she never showed.

The cyclone takes hold of the island and alters the whole ambience of the natural world and its people. The air is electric.

My keys jingle. I head out to the ambulance, a Mini Moke, and climb in. The canvas canopy doesn't include sides and the horizontal rain drenches me. I can barely make out the mud road. I turn toward the cliff. Somewhere in the heavy cloud the hospital perches, lit up sporadically by lightning. The howling wind wraps around like a suffocating blanket. The Mini Moke dodges the palms, deformed and bowed over the track.

Through the windscreen wipers I see the hospital backlit by a swinging kerosene lamp. Finally I park close in. Sue takes me to see our only patient, Carol. Sue is tired and says she'll come down when Carol goes into third-stage labour. She climbs the cliff to the nurses' quarters.

There is another storm brewing.

'Sorry, Carol, I'm a bit late. Thought I was going to be blown off the cliffs. How's the baby? Still stuck? Let's have a look.'

Carol is having her first baby. She has been in labour all day and we are concerned, as the babe is stuck in transverse position. We two are alone in the long tin building. An old woman died two days ago after she had been given the mandatory shower. We don't think it was the shower that killed her. She suffered from heart disease and TB. She was only in her fifties but she seemed very old. After she died, the women came to bash their heads with rocks and to wail, leaning on the veranda posts. The hospital was declared full of evil spirits and all the patients fled.

Except Carol: she knows where she and the baby are safest. Carol is married to an old man, forced on her by tribal law. She and most of her family, including her old husband, have leprosy. She is in remission because she regularly takes her medication. To complicate matters regarding her confinement, she has left her husband for Jim, the man she loves. This is a dangerous time. Babies have disappeared before and we are determined to keep this little one safe.

'Hope this storm passes soon,' Carol says. 'It makes me think of that night when my mother took me out to the island. I refused to marry the leprous old bastard. Ned already had my three sisters. Thought he stopped with Wendy. But no, he wanted me too. I hate the Promise System! Then my mother left me there with the old man. He raped me. The leprous old bastard raped me.'

Ned drives the night cart, swarmed over by a dozen or so of his little naked offspring. They always have infections, those kids. But they are cheery and cheeky. Once they reach six years old they go to school,

Night Journeys

so night carting with Papa is finished. But Ned's wives are an unhappy lot. The Promise System allows him all the daughters of one man who will in turn promise his daughters to another — in the same totem group. Ned has four sister-wives and the elder three make life miserable for Carol. She runs off with Jim, causing uproar on the island. They plan to leave by barge but Carol goes into labour and spoils the plan.

'Now the young men are standing up against the old men. Good on 'em,' she pants. 'Jim and I'll show 'em. Anyway, I've made my statement. I've left him and Jim is now my man. Where is he?'

Between contractions, Carol continues. 'You'd think Wendy would be on my side, being the youngest wife. She must remember what it's like. The new wife always gets beaten up.' With a lopsided smile she says, 'At least you lot know how to sew up split scalps.'

I nod. Sewing split scalps has become a frequent job for us nurses. Everyone here loves a fight and a funeral. We are the last call in the celebrations: stitching up broken faces in the former, and treating everyone for diarrhoea in the latter. You hear it before you see it: a circle of women with two wives tugging hair, scratching, skin tearing, kids whooping and cheering. You smell it before you see it: after sitting by the body, cooking in the sun for a week, most people in the vicinity end up at the hospital for plugging-up treatment.

Jim turns up and gives me time to retrieve Sue from her warm bed. This is secret women's business and men are not allowed to be within cooee. He comes to make plans for their escape and to encourage Carol. After a while he leaves, swallowed up by the storm. It's four am. The baby has turned head down, and contractions are coming at regular intervals.

With a prayer of thanks the little girl is born.

The storm passes.

Other storms still brew on the island.

The next morning the family flies to Darwin to begin a new life.

****

Chapter Eight

Hibiscus
Brighton (1972)

Arms entwined, we sit together on the end of the bed looking at the window. The hibiscus nods gracefully, pale pink petals, mid bright green, splayed against the glass. Bright pink stamens press forward, leaving a dusky swipe of yellow. Sunshine sparkles between gently waving blooms, filling the bedroom with light and beauty.

'Raylene, there's something I want to ask you,' says Mum quietly.

'Anything Mum, you know that,' I assure her warmly.

'It's a big 'ask'…I want you to take charge of my illness.'

'Mum, I wish you'd never have to ask! But, yes, of course I will. I'll stay with you and look after you in every way I can.'

'Good,' she says with a deep sigh… 'That's a big load off my shoulders.' Taking a big breath she continues: 'I've divided my life into four parts. The illness is one of them and you've taken responsibility for that, so that leaves three major areas to tackle and you've already begun one of them.'

'You mean my being useful; going through the kitchen, the laundry and painting the walls, cupboards…that sort of thing?'

'Yes,' Mum says, 'that sort of thing. Now I need to cull even more stuff from the kitchen to make things easier for the family.'

'Mum, we aren't giving up are we?'

'No dear, but let's face it. The prognosis is bad isn't it? I mean what can they do once it's got to the liver?'

My eyes start to fill up again, as my brave little mother continues: 'Now Raylene, no more crying in front of me, from now on. We'll cry privately.' She sighs and adds: 'I'll have to go through this with so many people.'

'I know.' I say with deep regret.

The previous day, while I was watching television with Stevie, while Dad read the paper, Mum walked into the room. Her face was pale grey in striking contrast to her aqua coloured dressing gown. She looked straight at me, her eyes large, bright, and confronting.

'Am I going to be here this time next year?'

'What?' I jump up from my seat.

'Am I going to be here this time next year?' Desperation enters her voice.

'Mum, I don't know if any of us will be here this time next year.' I answer evasively, as I move towards her.

'Then what was Joyce on about?' She speaks into my face, her usual calm voice overtaken by a note of panic.

'I don't know. Wasn't she just telling you about the Fete?' I say hopefully.

'Yes she was; telling me how well my stall went at the Babies Home Fete. I said to her: "Joyce, you're speaking as if I won't be here next year to over-see the Staff Stall". Joyce wouldn't look at me. So I said it again, and she got up and just raced out of the room and left the house. Raylene, what's happening?'

I looked around but Dad had left the room. Fourteen-year-old Stevie was still glued to the television and quite oblivious to the fact that his mother and sister were about to engage in a heartbreaking conversation. I gently lead her into the bedroom. Outside in my mother's garden, the hibiscus bends towards us.

****

Three months before, I was called to the phone where my brother David told me the devastating news that our mother had been given six months to live. During an operation, bowel cancer and overwhelming secondary cancer in the liver were discovered. There was no treatment for liver cancer in 1971. I was living in Sydney at the time with my husband Peter and our three-year-old son Mark-John.

'What does Mum say?' I ask anxiously.

'She doesn't know.'

'What?' I exclaim in disbelief.

'Dad said that she wasn't to be told.' David answers defensively. 'The doctors said that she would go through a time of improvement, now that the blockage in the bowel was dealt with, and that during that time she need not know the worst.'

'David, I can't believe this,' I say. 'It's not the way Mum would want it. She needs to know from the outset, it's her body and her life. We have talked about this, she and I, and I know she would be humiliated knowing that others knew about her condition before she did.'

'Dad wants it that way.' A note of desperation enters my poor brother's voice.

'That's because he can't face it.' I can only think of my mother.

'Dad warned me that you might not agree with him,' David declares, 'but he begs you to come and look after her when she comes out of hospital. And not let on.'

'You mean, lie to her,' I say indignantly.

'Mum is relieved that she doesn't have a colostomy.' David says, ignoring my last terse comment. 'That's what her father had, and he died.'

'I know.' I interrupt, fear taking hold of me.

'When Mum woke up from the surgery she said, "Have I got a colostomy?" And when told "no" she was reassured, and assumed that things were okay.'

Silence.

'Of course I'll come over and nurse her, but I don't know how I can pretend that the surgery is successful. How could I deceive her like that?'

'Do it for Dad's sake then,' David's voice softens.

'He's not the issue here.'

'Think about it.'

Night Journeys

I did more than think about it. I went off the pill and amazingly conceived a child immediately. I had a deep feeling that I wanted my mother to see and know this child. Perhaps I could keep her alive until after the birth! That didn't happen. I was only 20 weeks pregnant when Mum died, so she never saw her second grandson, James. I made plans to enable me to be with my mother for as long as she needed me. For three months I cared for her and the household, our initial conversation laying the framework for the months ahead.

'I'm so glad you're here.' Mum smiled. 'It's good of Peter to let you come and of course to have His Royal Highness around will brighten us all up.' Mark-John was already ruling the roost in the bungalow at Brighton.

'I'm here for as long as you need me, Mum. Peter is due to go on military exercises in Queensland next week for two months. Why stay in Sydney when we can be together here?' Lying came easy with such plausible excuses.

'When Doctor Magarey told me that I would need surgery to release the scar tissue after the gall bladder operation, I thought of my father,' Mum explained. 'I'd been in such pain so I said to myself, if I woke up with a colostomy, like he did, then I would have the same thing, cancer. But I didn't. The pain is better, so I must be getting better, eh?'

'That's great Mum. I can see how relieved you are,' I replied. 'Why not make the most of me while I'm here? Put me to all those odd jobs you haven't felt like doing these past months since your gall bladder op.'

And so she did. While Mum supervised and enjoyed her first grandchild's company, I got to work.

****

We walk into her room and sit on the end of the bed facing the Hibiscus.

'What's going on Raylene? What scared Joyce off? Why aren't I getting better?' Then a pause: 'Am I dying?'

The following conversation was so traumatic that I cannot remember my exact words, but somehow I answered her and told her what the doctors had discovered. Then Mum asked me how long she had.

'Six months they say, but there is no way they can really know.' I try to give an impression of the possibility of miscalculation on the doctors' part.

'Six months from the operation, or six months from now?' Mum looks straight ahead towards the window.

'Oh Mum, I'm so sorry. Six months from the operation.' I look down at my hands.

'What!' She exclaims. 'That means I've only three months left.' She turns to me and gives me a reproachful look, 'And you never told me.'

'I am so sorry Mum. I wanted to. But everyone else wanted to protect you for as long as possible.'

'Until Joyce couldn't hide it any more!'

'Yes.' I'm totally wiped out. I can't speak anymore. I want to howl.

'Raylene, would you please leave me for a while? When your Dad comes back, would you ask him to come in and see me?'

'Of course, Mum.' My reply is muffled as my hands cover my face. 'I am so sorry. I love you so much.' The false world that I have been living in these past three months is splintering. I wobble towards my bedroom where Mark-John is having his afternoon nap, and purge myself with tears.

That's how, the next day, we come to be sitting on the end of her bed planning strategies while watching the hibiscus gently swaying in the warm February breeze. The Venetian blinds have been pulled up, allowing the window to be filled with green and pink dyes, providing privacy, scent and beauty, screening everything that happens in Mum and Dad's bedroom from the outside world.

'I've been thinking.' My mother says. 'I have lived my life to glorify God and in my dying I want to do the same.'

We sit in silence. Then she says, 'I will divide my life into four sections. The first section is my relationship with God. That's intact and

I need no help with that.' Mum's well-thumbed Bible resting on her bedside table gives testament to her firm faith.

'The second section I have to do entirely on my own. It's the hardest part. It's dealing with the closest relationships in my life, Dad and Stevie, Nanna and the immediate family. Then there is everyone else. There are so many to say goodbye to and only I can do that.

'We've already begun the process of simplifying the housekeeping these past three months.' That's Mum's section three.

'And section four is the illness itself. Knowing that you will be here to nurse me covers that segment,' she adds, as if she is talking about the anatomy of an orange.

In less than twenty-four hours my amazing mother has come up with this approach to cope with the future. I am not surprised that my mother is thinking like this. She is the strongest person I know; able to draw on inner resources fired by her personal relationship with Jesus. I am ashamed that I have lied to Mum all these months. As predicted, Mum was humiliated to discover that everyone in the neighbourhood knew of her condition.

'I used to wonder why people gave me strange looks and tended to break off conversations with me.' Mum mused. 'And Joyce was the last straw. That's why I challenged her, poor thing. I'd better get a message to her to come and see me.' She continued, after a brief pause: 'Oh dear, I'm going to have to reach out to so many who have been worried about me.'

Mum commences to comfort her family and friends. They come away from her amazed and humbled that she could face this major traumatic event with such courage and assurance.

****

It was during this time Mum found me weeping on my bed. She sat down next to me and gently placed her hand upon my shoulder, 'Don't cry my dear; don't cry for me.'

I turned and faced her and uttered the shameful words: 'Mum, I'm not crying for you, I am crying for me. You have the love of your husband and all your family around you. You know where you are going, and most of all, your husband, my Dad, loves you dearly. I don't know that sort of love and if I were in your place, my husband would find all the excuses in the world not to be with me. I'm crying because I have never been loved like you. I'm crying for myself.'

She laid her head near mine. 'My dear daughter, I know it's been difficult for you. But marriage has to be worked on. It wasn't always easy for your Dad and me. After the war we had years with your dad suffering from war neurosis.'

'Yes I know. I remember when he was healed,' I said. 'I was fourteen. But I was never fearful that you didn't love each other.'

'Still, it was hard.' Mum is quiet for a moment. 'Your father is the only man I have ever loved.'

'And you are the only woman he has ever loved, Mum. I hate what is happening to you. Dad is devastated and Stevie cannot comprehend it.'

****

Easter came and went, and I took Mark-John back to Sydney to spend some time with his father. I was almost half way through my pregnancy. My younger sister Lesley and my brother's wife Gill used the school holidays to care for Mum for the two weeks. They took turns at being on call and seventy-four-year-old Nanna Bowey continued to cook dainty dishes daily for her daughter to encourage her to eat.

Then ten days into our break, Mum's condition deteriorated overnight. She was unable to breathe without help, and in acute pain. Mark-John and I returned to a very different scene.

****

'What's that doing there?' I point to the oxygen cylinder beside Mum's bed.

'I have to use it every time I move, or whenever someone does anything for me.'

'You won't need that anymore,' I say quietly, 'now I'm here.' I wheel the monster out of the room.

'I'm so glad you're back.' Sighing deeply, Mum manages a weak smile, her huge eyes sunken; the planes of her face skeletal. 'I feel better already.' After a moment she says with apprehension: 'I'm worried about Mark-John seeing me. I made little Andrew from next-door cry when Cynthia brought him in to see me the other day. I look so dreadful.'

'You needn't worry about your grandson.' I say confidently of the little boy who adores his Nanna. 'He's asleep now but he'll see you in the morning and I guarantee that he will be so excited to see you…..he won't notice…..' My voice drops, 'How you've changed.' I hold Mum gently. Then as I sit up, I turn and look straight into the mirror!

'And the second thing we're going to do is move that thing.' I indicate the dressing table with the huge round mirror positioned so that every time Mum sits up she is confronted with her concentration camp inmate reflection.

'Oh please do, Raylene. I've wanted to ask for it to be moved since I had the collapse, but I didn't want to upset anyone.'

I go to my distraught Dad sitting with his head in his hands in the kitchen, a cold cup of tea before him. Between us we drag the huge piece of furniture away from their bed. Already Mum's ravaged face looks more relaxed.

The next morning three year old Mark-John bounds into his Nanna's room.

'I'm back Nanna!'

He's everything his mother expects him to be. Seeing his Nanna for who she truly is, not for what she looks like.

****

The second quarter of her life is, as she expected, the hardest to bear. Mum has said goodbye to everyone she knows and now her personal world is shrinking. Major events no longer interest her; only the hibiscus shares this time of precious intimacy. The small circle of her family and her own body fill her consciousness, and every afternoon fourteen year old Stephen sits at his mother's bedside and does his homework.

'Norm Hayward has just rung, Mum.' I come into her sun-lit room. 'He asks if you'd like him to come and give you Holy Communion.'

'I'd like that,' she replies, sinking back into the pillows. Mum has been bedridden since the collapse. 'Ask him to come tomorrow when Nanna is here. We'll celebrate it together.'

We three women and the minister take the bread and wine and sit quietly. This is the body of Christ given for you. The blood of Christ shed for the forgiveness of your sins. We are in the sublime presence. Nanna needs comfort too. She is facing every parent's nightmare, to have their child die before them. Mum is only fifty-two and Nanna will live another twenty years.

****

It is the May school holidays and all the immediate family are around the house, except Dad who reluctantly goes to work each day.

'I'm afraid pneumonia has set in. I think we should admit her.' Dr Magarey states what I am dreading to hear, but prepared to fight about.

'No!' I am emphatic. 'Mum and I have discussed it.'

The doctor and I are standing in the garden after his examination of my dying mother.

I continue, 'In the beginning of her illness she wouldn't consider dying at home. She thought it would be too upsetting for the family. You remember that, Doctor?'

He nods in agreement. I go on, 'Now she knows going into hospital is the worst thing to do for everyone, including herself. We're all in this together.' And flinging my arms around, 'Even her beloved garden shares this time.'

Dr Magarey watches me closely.

'She has the best nursing possible and her pain is minimal. I haven't even had to use the Pethidine or the oxygen.' I add to reassure him: 'If we can't cope, I'll let you know.'

****

Looking back, I consider the time I had to tell Mum that she was dying the most distressing conversation I had ever had. But that night, Mum, stroking my expanding stomach, and talking about the grandchild she would never see, whispered words that broke my heart. She was recalling the Holy Communion we had shared that afternoon and how Jesus faced the Garden of Gethsemane experience. Now, she faced hers. My mother's large brown eyes looked intently into mine, her face wizened through the ravages of the disease that was taking her from us.

'I never thought… it was going to be… this hard.' She whispered. 'Could there have been… another way?' While I held onto her tiny hand, my throat closing up, she paused and said: 'Never-the-less…Thy will be done.'

It wasn't until the next afternoon that I realised the special timing of that disclosure.

****

Raylene Pearce

Everything changes the next day. I give her an afternoon wash and some morphia and aspirin mixture, and make sure she is comfortable. Dad has only just left to go back to work after lunch and I will never forget his weeping, on his knees with his head beside his wife, as he cries:

'Don't leave me Marj, don't leave me. Please get well. I love you so much.'

A few minutes after going to my bed to rest for the night shift, my sister-in-law comes in to say that Mum has stopped breathing. I enter my mother's bedroom. Nanna is sitting in the chair beside the silent form of her only daughter and I know as I walk in that my mother's spirit has left her. We stand looking at her peaceful face and gaze in wonder: such a wonderful wife, a caring daughter, a marvellous mother, mother-in-law and grandmother, and dear friend to many people.

I go outside into the garden, pick a pale pink hibiscus, and place it in my mother's still hand.

****

The cords of death entangled me;
the torrents of destruction overwhelmed me.
In my distress I called to the LORD;
I cried to my God for help.
He reached down from on high
and took hold of me;
he drew me out of deep waters.
He brought me out into a spacious place;
He rescued me because he delighted in me.

Psalm 18: verses 4,6,16,19

Chapter Nine

Night Sea Journey
Papua New Guinea (1981)

Lord take me now!
I cannot bear it.
Take me now.

A sharp retort.
One son speaks to the other
playing cards on the bunk above my bier
over the noise of the waves
on the open top deck
of the Lutheran Shipping Line
south of Finschhafen
where two great tides meet.
Five women, and eight children
on top, with the waves washing over.
Booked seats!

Lord, Take me now
I cannot bear it.
Take me now.

I disappear into the ice cream carton.
Up comes lunch, or maybe breakfast.
There go our cases again
first to the left then swish to the right.

Raylene Pearce

Will they return?
All our luggage overboard.
The other passengers,
many local people, goats and pigs,
knowing a thing or two,
didn't book seats.
They took their chance
and now shelter safely below.

A leg appears. A face.
James looks into mine as it rises white
above the ice cream carton.
'You ok mum? Is there anything to eat?'
'Awwwwwwww.' Into the carton I go.
I can't even feed my young.
What good am I?
If we sink, I'll be no good to anyone
All I want is to die.

Lord, Take me now
I cannot bear it.
Take me now.

Five women friends from Lae,
with a great idea to take our children, to
Finschhafen, on the north-east point
of Papua New Guinea.
First, the historic house was the Lutheran Mission.
Invading Japanese requisitioned it as the Pacific HQ.
After victory, it became the Allied Forces Hospital.
And after the war,
returned to the Lutherans
and reincarnated as a Guest House.

Night Journeys

The day before we left Lae in flat calm.
I, glued to the railing,
took photos of cheery faces,
the children filled with excitement.
Even the mothers!
What if we go under?
When a woman has lost her ability to save her children
she might as well die.
I ask God one more time to answer my prayer –

Take me now,
I cannot bear it.
He refuses.

Nothing changes except the time.
At three a.m. we enter Finshchhafen harbour.
It's raining, the jetty deserted
like a scene in a horror film.
Nothing to see but rain.
Nothing to feel but rain
and gratitude, as the land heaves
and my stomach stops.

Someone's awake.
A truck, with shrouded sound, emerges, piercing the veil
and takes us jolting through the jungle
winding upwards on a scarred white track.
A light appears beside a door.
We drag our cases and stand in the lobby like refugees
dripping in the Lutheran Mission Station.
Home for the next week for five mothers and
eight children.

Raylene Pearce

Nothing to dread but the trip back!
This time in the bowels of the boat,
with goats, and hens and the smell of diesel.

Lord…..please!

****

The Keeping Grace of God

Although I was a Christian, and the Holy Spirit was present in me, it wasn't till I was in the death throes of my marriage while in Papua New Guinea that I was released in the Spirit.
Let me tell you how that happened.
It was in the October of 1982 and I had been lying in bed composing a letter to my father-in-law telling him how he had been the cause of my husband's rejection of me. Earlier, not long after I met my husband, he had rejected my husband's mother, and history was repeating itself.
I got up and sat in the living room, the Papua-New Guinea moonlight coming through the slatted windows. As I sat there I started to feel ashamed of my thoughts and noticed a small book on the coffee table, written by James Dobson. I flipped through it and read: 'God will not lead you where the Spirit will not keep you.' I thought that wasn't a helpful thing and thought that God had surely not led me to this place where my husband had publicly rejected me.
Now I was on my knees before the coffee table and something came over me. From out of my mouth, from the depth of my heart, came words that my Heavenly Father had been waiting to hear from me for a long time, three words:

Night Journeys

'I've botched it!'

As soon as my confession was out of my mouth the Holy Spirit fell on me and for some hours I was in the Spirit and felt waves of God's love flood over me.

During this time I started to pray in a strange language. It sounded to my ears like a Middle European language. It seemed to me that there was a woman trying to pray, a woman unable to pray from where she was, maybe behind the Iron Curtain. The prayer continued for what seemed a long, long time. I felt that the Lord was using me as a conduit for this captive woman's prayers. I had never had such an experience before. When finally the intercession ended I returned to bed just as the dawn broke and I realised that I had been in the living room for at least four hours!

The following day the devil spoke to me. 'You don't need this stuff, Raylene. You are such a good person. You are the hurt one in this marriage.'

But, resisting him, I went into my bedroom after the family had left for work and school, and got down on my knees again and prayed, 'Please Father, tell me what happened last night?'

I waited, then a song started and I sang in another unknown tongue, but this time it wasn't a human language, but seemed like one of angels.

After a while I asked again, 'Please Father, tell me what I have just sung. Tell me in English, so I won't think I'm going off my head.' And almost before that prayer was spoken I started to sing in English.

> "Hallelujah, Hallelujah my God I see.
> My King is in heaven
> His Spirit in me."

And several verses like this.

Raylene Pearce

Then I went to visit a Christian friend, Barbara Cook, who lived down the street. I went into her house and sat down on the kitchen stool and just sat there. She waited and she waited. She was waiting for the next episode of 'Raylene's miserable marriage'. I was dumb. I had nothing to say. Actually from that day onwards I have had nothing more to say about my marriage in a negative way to anyone. And it occurred to me that God had granted me two gifts: the gift of tongues and the gift of 'shut up'!

Even though I felt a changed person, my husband never noticed and insisted we go our separate ways.

We did so at Adelaide Airport.

****

How long, O LORD? Will you forget me forever?
How long will you hide your face from me?
How long must I wrestle with my thoughts
and every day have sorrow in my heart?

But I trust in your unfailing love;
my heart rejoices in your salvation.
I will sing to the LORD,
for he has been good to me.

A psalm of David 13 v1, 2, 4, 5

Chapter Ten

Shame Suffering (1993)

I was so ashamed that I couldn't make my marriage work like a Christian woman should. I felt like I was going into the night journey of the soul. The shame was palpable. I was so surprised, when looking back at photographs from that time of the return, that I looked so ordinary. My family and friends treated me kindly but inside I felt all screwed up.

Two years before, the boys and I had been sent off from Coromandel Valley Uniting Church with prayers and prophecy that my marriage would heal away from all the family grief we had suffered. We had lost 17 people from our family in 17 years by the time our marriage was truly over. This included both our mothers from cancer and my younger brother, Stephen, aged 18, after playing cricket for Glenelg, killed by a drunk driver.

Peter told me as he left us in Adelaide to take up his posting in Victoria, 'If there hadn't been so many deaths, we might have made it.'

I hadn't counted the deaths in Vietnam of twenty-year old boys under his charge. Where do you go with grief like that if you have rejected God's love? My father had accepted 'The One who carries our fears and sorrows' and he and Mum were happily married until Mum's untimely death at the age of 52.

To return to your church a failed person is a great trauma, a deep dark place where you feel deserving of condemnation. It's one thing to endure a dying marriage privately but to be left to face everyone as a rejected woman in the public place is excruciating.

But I will never forget that day. We worshipped in the little hundred and thirty four year old Church on the corner of Ackland Hill and

Main Road, Coromandel Valley. As usual it was packed. People stood outside by the long windows to listen until the children moved out to their Sunday school classes. Then the rest of the congregation took their seats.

The Reverend Arthur Jackson saw me and he called me to the front and welcomed me back and prayed for us as we faced a new future. Then at the end of the service he asked me to come and stand with him at the door so I could greet everyone! Can you imagine it? How would you feel? What love is this? I was enfolded into the community of faith, and Coromandel Valley Uniting Church has been my heart place of worship ever since.

Not long after that, Helen Hayman rang. 'Raylene,' she said, 'can you come back on the Prayer Chain?'

I was gobsmacked. 'Why would you ask me to do that?'

'We want you to pray about it.'

'Helen. Thank you. I can't. I've too much to work through and a new life to face. But thanks so much for asking me. Please ask my friends to pray for me.'

That invitation went a long way in the healing of the hurt of rejection and the perception of disgrace.

The new life included finding a house we could afford, getting a job, trying to help the boys through all this and re-connecting with friends made four years before when we first came to Coromandel Valley in 1979. Facing the future meant feeling utterly inadequate and scared.

Two weeks before the end of the Christmas holidays Ray and Betty Elford, friends of mine since I was twelve when Betty taught me at Hamilton Park Sunday School, found a house for us in their street. The cottage was ours if we wanted it. We sure wanted it! School was to begin and I jumped at the opportunity to be near the boys' schools and our church.

For the four years we lived in the cottage, we grew in faith as we were loved and guided by our church family. We were taught the deep truths of the faith and participated in spiritual renewal with vibrant worship, prayer, and care for each other. Youth Group, youth camps, Mark-John in the band *Soul Purpose,* women's share group, House group, and Charismatic Conventions became integral to our life.

Rod James became our new minister when Arthur retired and he arranged mentors for Mark-John and James, and oversaw the ministry of the *Overcomers* who met in our home. This ministry, raised by God, helped stop me from becoming a self-pitying mess. He gave me wonderful women friends facing challenges within and without marriage. We gathered each Wednesday to support and to reinforce our knowing that in Jesus we could overcome all obstacles.

At the same time I began work with *The Company.* Another gift from a Heavenly Father who knew that as our little family shrunk (divorced people know what I'm saying). He gave us an international family for the next 22 years!

During these years the Lord gave me Isaiah 54 v 4-8.

Here are some of the verses that helped me through the difficult time.

****

'Do not be afraid; you will not suffer shame.
Do not fear disgrace; you will not be humiliated.
You will forget the shame of your youth
and remember no more the reproach of your widowhood.
For your Maker is your husband –
The LORD almighty is his name.
The LORD will call you back as if you were
a wife deserted and distressed in spirit
- a wife who married young,
- only to be rejected' says your God.

Chapter Eleven

Nanna and the Good Shepherd

In 1983 Grandpa Bowey died at the age of 98. For four more years Nanna and I would share our special times but she was now frail and in her mid nineties. Sitting together in the sunroom of the elderly citizen's hostel in which she now lived we would have these conversations:

'I'm looking forward to meeting my two husbands in heaven.'

'Yes, that'll be good.'

'They were best friends you know. Charles made Rupert promise to look after me, but of course Rupert had a wife then.'

'Yes, that was a bit inconvenient. But wonderful that you were able to care for their girls during her final illness.'

'She was very nice, but she caught me darning Rupert's socks one day and accused me of having an affair with him! She went berserk!'

On another visit Nanna seemed preoccupied and worried.

'Raylene, I don't think Jesus loves me any more.' She looked around at the nodding ladies in the bright, but awfully quiet, sunroom.

'Now why would you say that?'

'Look at all these women he's got to contend with!'

'Oh, I think he can manage.'

Silence. Then her face lit up.

'Now I remember.'

'Yes Jesus loves me, Yes Jesus loves me,
Yes Jesus loves me. The Bible tells me so.'

She sang as she turned her face to the setting sun.

****

Night Journeys

I sense it the moment I wake up. This will be our final day together. I go to Nanna.

****

I climb in. The bed is narrow and hard, her tiny frame, bird-like. I settle down beside her, my dark head against the pillow, her silver one resting in the crook of my arm.

Uncle Ken, Nanna's son, and Aunty Audrey are sitting beside her bed.

I begin to sing. Nanna and I have sung so many songs before. This time she just lies like a little baby encircled in my arms.

> *'The Lord's my Shepherd, I'll not want,*
> *He makes me down to lie*
> *In pastures green, He leadeth me*
> *The quiet waters by.'*

Now I hold my precious Nanna as she held me as a child. Comforting me when I was upset, tickling me just to hear me chortle and choke, and snuggling up with me in expectation of the wonders that would flow out of the soft golden glow of the mantel radio. I sing each verse through. I come to the final verse:

> *'Goodness and mercy all my life*
> *Will surely follow me.*
> *And in God's house for evermore,*
> *My dwelling place shall be'.*

As the song ends, my Nanna, Jessie Bowey, aged 96, gives a tiny sigh and slips into *God's house for evermore.*

Silence.

****

Raylene Pearce

I feel no grief, just floods of grateful memory, of goodness and mercy in the life of a woman who helped form my world view, that this life is not all that there is.
 Aunty Audrey leans forward her eyes wide and says, 'I never thought it would be like this.'

****

And now dear brothers and sisters,
I want you to know what happens to a Christian when they die
so that when it happens, you will not be full of sorrow,
as those are who have no hope.
For since we believe that Jesus died and then came back to life again,
we can also believe that when Jesus returns,
God will bring back with him all the Christians who have died.

1 Thessalonians 4 v 13, 14

The Living Bible,
Tyndale House Publishers 1976 Wheaton, Illinois

Chapter Twelve

The Tale of Two Houses
(1983 – 1988)

I want to tell you about our little house of the corner of Sturt Ave and Sussex Street, Hawthorndene.

After the soldiers returned home from the First World War, they were given land, and many built their homes like they had seen in France.

In the case of our house, imagine a pile of large rocks as a foundation. Large wooden posts dropped into each corner. Tightly strained double chicken wire tautly spread between. This created a narrow space for hay to be packed in. Onto this structure stucco was plastered on the outside and plywood on the inside walls. This formed two bedrooms, a tiny kitchen, and an L shaped living and dining room. Later a small bathroom, laundry, and a lean-to louvre-windowed third bedroom were added to complete the cottage.

It looked grotty, but we made it into a cosy, homely dwelling where for four years the boys and I lived. I used to delight in telling visitors how well our home was made. After all it was still standing since 1919. I would lead them outside around the side of the house. They were invited to look into a small hole in the north-facing wall of the living room and there they could see the chicken wire and bright yellow hay!

At one time we had rats from the nearby creek scurrying up inside the walls, possums bouncing in the roof space, mice under the floorboards. At one time a hive of bees set up home beside my bedroom window. A very lively house indeed!

Raylene Pearce

That was the end of December 1982.
On May 10th 1983 I received a phone call. 'I'm going to start divorce proceedings.'
I was stunned and managed to ask why, as we had arranged a year separation. He had no explanation. That day was also the tenth anniversary of my mother's death and the first day of starting my new job with *The Company*. I felt like I had been bashed in the stomach. This news began eighteen months of being in limbo (neither married nor un-married) until the day after my, happy to forget fortieth birthday when the *decree absolute* came in the post.
During those years I did all sorts of fitness things – jazz ballet with Helen Magarey and mother's netball for Coro Primary School. To make up for a great deficit in my childhood (never having ever roller-skated) I decided to learn. So there I was gazing up at the Mother's Roller-skating Classes on the notice board of the Blackwood Recreation Centre. From the corner of my eye I noticed a woman doing the same. We both turned to each other. Our eyes opened wide and so did our mouths.
'Margaret!' said I.
'Raylene!' said Margaret.
We grabbed onto each other. Margaret and I had been best friends at Brighton High School and had not seen or heard from each other for twenty years! When you meet a friend after a long time, maybe because you have aged at the same rate you recognise each other. Margaret with her short naturally curly light brown hair, slender build, and lovely eyes looked the same to me. I'm not sure about me, though, and what colour my hair was that day!
When we were students we used to spend our lunch times reading, reading and reading. Except in the summer if we were quick and got a tennis court. On leaving school, Margaret worked at the Bank of Adelaide and I trained at the Memorial Hospital. Then we lost touch.
And here we were enrolling in Mother's Roller-skating class at Blackwood Recreation Centre, both married with two boys a-piece.

Night Journeys

She and John Beaumont had been translating the scriptures, with the Summer Institute of Linguistics in Papua New Guinea for many years. We were in Adelaide on compassionate posting because of Peter's mother's illness and death and other tragedies happening in our lives. They were on furlough from Papua New Guinea. We were waiting to move to Canberra for our next posting.

Then during lesson two I managed to tear the ligament on my left knee roller-skating with a broom! It was Margaret who took me to the physiotherapist. During this time we visited each other's houses, both in Coromandel Valley. I remember helping her plant rhododendrons along the back garden over-looking the valley.

Then came the day we said goodbye and were really sad. Margaret left to stay with in-laws at Victor Harbor en route to Ukurumpa in the highlands of Papua New Guinea.

That very day Peter came home from Keswick Barracks and asked, 'What would you think about not going to Canberra next posting, but to PNG?'

I nearly jumped out of my skin with delight and raced to phone Margaret at the Beaumont relatives in Victor with the news.

A month later we packed up the house on Main Road and stayed with church friends John and Beryl Skewes on Ackland Hill Road for several weeks. In the New Year we moved to Lae in Morobe Province to live in Igham barracks. I remember visiting John Beaumont in Angua hospital when he had dengue fever. This was to be the last two years of my marriage.

****

Why do I tell this tale?

Because four years after moving into the house of straw, chicken wire, and stone, we were introduced to our next home in the form of a vision.

Raylene Pearce

Our minister, Rod James, was having a meal with us while his wife Shirley was visiting family in New Zealand.

Just as he was about to leave, he said, 'You'll be moving from here very soon. This house is not safe. It's a fire trap.'

Then he proceeded to describe the house that we would move to. 'It's a fine house with long windows looking out over the valley. It has lots of light and space.'

That was the Wednesday. On Saturday our landlord Ron came around to collect the rent. He looked shame-faced and stood in front of me and said, 'I've some bad news Raylene.'

'Oh,' I said, 'You want us to move?'

Ron's eyes widened. 'How'd know?'

'Rod told us.'

'How could he know?' said the incredulous landlord. 'We only decided last night to prepare this block for building!'

Here we were again, homeless.

The following day my friend Mary May came over to have a prayer time with the boys and me. Shortly after we started to pray about the need for a new home, the phone rang.

Mark-John took it. 'It's Papua New Guinea, Mum,' he cried.

I held out my hand.

'Is that you, Ray? Do you need a house?' It was John Beaumont!

In Ukurumpa in the highlands of Papua New Guinea, Marg and John were praying about the fact that their tenant had to make an emergency move to Queensland. John's brother was to put an advert in the Advertiser newspaper the following Saturday.

'As we prayed about it, your name came to our minds. And we were also to offer you a reduction off the rent.'

This was so remarkable. Up till then six people from our church were supporting us. Ray Elford would then give the money to me to help pay the rent. I'll never forget those people, Ray and Betty, David and Judy, and Kay and Shirley.

Night Journeys

What a faith boost for us all! To know that at the same time we were both praying for the same thing. One prayer group, in Ukurumpa in PNG, and one in Hawthorndene, South Australia. And Rod had given a word of knowledge that we were to move, and that our landlord had confirmed it.

In five days the next stage of our lives was set. We were to move into a large and airy home, full of light streaming though the floor-to-ceiling windows that looked out into our beloved valley.

God was teaching me many things about trusting Him. This was a foretaste of the provision I would see when I was moving as a volunteer to the Middle East and raising Team Support.

And we moved into the house of the vision facing the east side of the valley.

We could see thick stands of eucalyptus with patches of flat open land and tiny brown and white cows, their heads bent to the grass. Towards the north, the forest of fir trees added a deeper shade of green and a landscape for the local boys to play in. The grey and white of the immense gums stretched to the sky, their branches filling the space all round.

Raylene Pearce

And for two winters I saw the rhododendrons bloom.
The very flowers I helped Margaret plant six years before.

****

Lord, you have assigned me my portion and my cup;
you have made my lot secure.
The boundary lines have fallen for me in pleasant places;
surely I have a delightful inheritance.

Psalm of David no 16 verses 5 & 6

Chapter Thirteen

The Old Stove
(1993)

I have had the privilege of speaking at conferences and meetings in many places. Just before I left for the Middle East I was the Mission Spot speaker for the *Christian Women Communicating International* weekend at Victor Harbor in South Australia. I had five minutes, and this is something of what I said… with an added bit.

****

Once I thought I was an old stove. You know the kind you see on the back veranda of old houses. There they stand, gathering cobwebs, rust, and the neighbour's displeasure.

I remember just such a stove at a house on Main Road, Coromandel Valley. As I drove past, I would quickly look to the left, and there it was for all to see – on the veranda an old stove, plunked beside an old sofa with the stuffing falling out.

I used to think, 'Yes, there you are, just like me. I bet there's a new model where you once were. A shiny, clean, sparkling stove, probably fan-forced and…self-cleaning!'

This happened many years ago at the time I was traded in for a new model wife. I truly thought I was like that old stove.

But I want to bear testimony to the One who is my Redeemer, Jesus. He rescues and reconditions old stoves. Not only that, but he restores them so completely that the inside is as sparkling clean as a brand-new model straight from the warehouse.

All he wants from us is a repentant heart and a willingness to be changed into something new, something the Father can use for his glory.

God never wastes anything. Nothing from the past is beyond restoration.

God cannot change the past, but he can change the way we respond to the past - now! We are not victims! We are Overcomers! How are we Overcomers? How do we overcome those things that torment us, that rise up and make us remember the dark things?

Because God is love, he brings us into his embrace and restores all the old stoves and all the young stoves whose shiny surfaces can be so easily scratched.

I want to paint you a picture of perfect love:

There never was a time when the Father was not the Father and there never was a time that the Son was not the Son. There was never a time when the Father did not love the Son and there was never a time when the Son did not love the Father. The third person of the Trinity, the Holy Spirit is equally placed in that love relationship of the three in One: the Father, the Son, and the Holy Spirit all in the community of love. There is a continual dance of love between them. The whole reason for their being is to love.

What is absolutely wonderful about all this is that the Triune God, that is, the Holy Trinity, has chosen to include us all in this wonderful overflowing love relationship. So as we believe in Him we are taken up into this embrace. That's what being a Christian means, being in relationship with God the Father, with Christ the Son, through the power of the Holy Spirit. Perfect love.

Before the world came to be, the God of love had already set up the plan, the great rescue plan that would include every person. You are not on planet earth by chance. God has a divine appointment with each of us. So he became one of us. Wore our skin, lived the life of a child and a young man. He said, 'I and the Father are One.' John 10 v 30.

Night Journeys

Two thousand years ago on a rock outside the city of Jerusalem, in the rubbish dump no less, this young man of thirty-three years was nailed to a cross and took into himself all that separates us from God and separates us from living a totally fulfilling life in God – now!

What happened on the cross releases us from being tied to the dreadfulness of past things. Jesus has taken into himself all the sin and suffering, all the abuse and loneliness, all the grief and sorrow. All that has hurt us, all the hurtful things that we have done to others, all that has broken us and our families, all that continues to hurt us and keeps us from living the abundant life. All this Jesus has taken away.

Like a sponge he soaked up all the sin for all time, for all people, and declared it defeated. 'It is finished,' cried out the young man in triumph. He had completed the work he had been sent to do: to defeat the works of the evil one, who tries to have control of our lives.

Something else he does, once we have asked for forgiveness and submitted to his loving hand. He remodels us, then sends us on our way. To stop me from feeling sorry for myself – you know, 'Poor me, no one loves me, no one claims me for his own, what a failure,' etc – he brought people who ministered to me and with whom I could share and to whom I could minister. He also placed me near stronger women who became my mentors and helpers.

Within months after Jesus had begun his healing work on me, He sent me on the most amazing adventure. Even as I was cast out of my marriage, He cast me in a job with a missionary organisation (which I am here calling *The Company*) and for twelve years I ran the office in Adelaide while bringing up my two boys.

So what does that mean to us?

It means that all old stoves can be restored and remodelled and that all young stoves can find the only safe place to be transformed in. It means that not one of us need leave this page, unhealed, broken, or beaten. All so-called victims will be made Overcomers by what Jesus has done for them.

Raylene Pearce

His completed work releases us all from the tyranny of the past, the present, and the future.
And who knows? He just might give you a future like mine - and send you to the ends of the earth!

****

After that address I was besieged by dozens of women, women who themselves felt like old stoves, or women whose daughters were going through divorce and rejection. What a time of healing prayer and celebration!
No longer stuck in past failure, but released where healing dwells - in the future, for the future.

****

Now to him who is able to do immeasurably more
than all we ask or imagine,
according to the power that is at work within us,
to him be glory in the church and in Christ Jesus
throughout all generations, for ever and ever! Amen.

Ephesians: 3 v 20

Part Three

Asia

Chapter Fourteen

Tears of the Women
Thailand (1986)

I'm in a hotel room in the south of Thailand. I'm convulsed with tears. I cannot stop crying. I don't know why. I randomly open my Bible and I read:

My eyes will flow unceasingly, without relief,
until the Lord looks down from heaven and sees.
What I see brings grief to my soul,
because of all the women of my city.

I've opened to the book of Lamentations, Chapter three.
 I go to the window and see a row of men leaning against their Hondas along the opposite side of the street. At intervals a young woman comes out of the hotel and engages in an altercation with a man. Then she is pushed back across the road to our hotel.
 During the one night we spend there I keep going to the door to stop it being knocked in. We can't work it out. Even standing at the window I'm unable to perceive what is going on. I just keep weeping.
 The following day, Sunday, we think we'll go to church. 'Church gave up long ago,' is the reply to our question.
 I'm traveling in Malaysia with friends, Jan Hepworth and Joan Brown, and staying in Penang. It's September 1986 and we take a service taxi, heading north along the Malay Peninsula to explore south-

ern Thailand. The limo we travel in is filled with Malaysian men who keep leering at us and talking about us with their heads nodding. We have no idea what we are traveling into.

A tourist brochure describes Hat Yai as good for souvenirs and entertainment facilities. We have come for the former but what is the latter? We notice the streets are filled with hundreds of beautiful girls, unlike other Asian streets that are filled mainly with men. As we enter various shops we notice that the girls serving us are not as glamorous as these other women. The shop girls are of shorter stature with gentle faces. We observe this before we understand the system of life and commerce in the city.

That day we discover the entire city of Hat Yai is a brothel. The households are mainly made up of at least three generations of female prostitutes. The brothers train as their pimps. The girls usually go on the streets at ten or eleven years of age and retire at twenty-one. Then they are married off to perpetuate the family business. Their less exotic sisters go to work in the tourist shops run by their fathers. Male Western and Asian sex tourists perpetuate the businesses.

I have a memory that will never let me go. As we walked along the packed narrow footpaths we passed something that made me take a second look. On the ground was a woman. She had no arms or legs. A little bell was attached to her shoulders and every now and then she would shrug and the bell would tinkle. A begging bowl sat in front of her and I am ashamed as I remember that I stumbled on. I couldn't deal with such an image. This was a real woman and I couldn't look at her.

On her return to Australia, Jan sent Thai Bibles to three girls working in a pottery shop.

Many years after our visit, a friend who was living in Thailand told me that the church had returned to Hat Yai, bringing hope to the women of the city.

****

Raylene Pearce

"O afflicted city, lashed by storms and not comforted,
I will build you with stones of turquoise,
your foundations with sapphires.

I will make your battlements of rubies,
your gates of sparkling jewels,
and all your walls of precious stones.

All your sons will be taught by the LORD,
and great will be your children's peace.

In righteousness you will be established:
Tyranny will be far from you;
you will have nothing to fear.

Terror will be far removed;
it will not come near you.

If anyone does attack you, it will not be my doing;
whoever attacks you will surrender to you.

no weapon forged against you will prevail,
and you will refute every tongue that accuses you.

This is the heritage of the servants of the LORD,
and this is their vindication from me."

declares the LORD.

Isaiah 54 v 11 - 15 & v

Chapter Fifteen

Life offers us gems. A handful of quartz scooped up in the White Desert of the Sahara at first looks dull but as the sun strikes each slither, the crystal releases light from the past.

For me, in 1999, to be considering moving into the flat on the first floor of the apartment in Cairo was informed by past hospitality I received in Nepal in 1991 while visiting partners serving there.

****

Hospitality
Nepal (1991)

The padded shoulders of our thick parkas brush the sides of the narrow passage. This leads to a ladder, our first climb between floors that seem packed like stacks of fish boxes in a warehouse.

Dennis's torch outlines the blue-painted door at the end of the ladder and he gently knocks. A young woman welcomes us and we step in. We enter a room bare except for the bedrolls on which we are to sit, with a black-and-white television set in the corner displaying battle scenes of a war movie with Hindi voiceover. We are left alone.

Because these tiered families are not wealthy, Dennis has suggested that each level in the house give a small course of a traditional welcoming meal. Even though it is a new idea to them, because they trust Dennis, they agree. This enables me to meet them and hear their stories without adding undue expense for them and embarrassment for us.

Raylene Pearce

'*Nameste.*'
Soon a young woman arrives with two eggs on tiny tin plates. While Dennis and I crack and eat the eggs, the family sit around us, watching and chatting, smiling and making me feel terrible. What if this is the only food they have?

Next we go higher and climb to the mother-in-law's residence and she presents us with a wheat mixture that sticks to the sides and roof of my mouth. Through gritty teeth we bow our thanks, say our goodbyes and proceed even higher.

Finally we come to the family with whom we are to spend the rest of the evening, a widow with one son and three daughters. Dennis met the young man at one of the ubiquitous coffee shops of Kathmandu. They pose for photographs with me. They sing, chat, and ask questions about me. All the time their TV is showing war movies.

'This family,' Dennis explains, 'is celebrating the rescue of their youngest daughter kidnapped by dacoits.' He goes on to explain. 'Dacoit gangs in India run drugs, conduct contract killings and prostitution rackets. This family of three daughters is the latest to be savaged by them. It's an expanding trade that feeds Christian Nepali virgins to the brothels of India.'

Asha, the mother, arrives with a small bowl of crushed wheat porridge and some spicy milk chai. Dennis greets her and introduces me. Soon Asha returns with Basanti, the rescued one.

The story told that night amazes me:

When Basanti was taken, their church in Kathmandu held all-night prayer vigils while Narayan, the brother, took the bus south to find his sister. He believed she had been taken to Old Delhi. After many days wandering the winding streets, he was on the point of giving up.

In despair, he found himself in a dark alley. His heart started to pump at an alarming rate and sweat broke out on his forehead. Something caused him to look up. As he did, his sister looked out of a tiny window. It can only be described as a miracle. He rushed into the apartment house, raced up the stairs, kicked in the door, and dragged Basanti away from her minder, an old woman, who was in charge of grooming her for her new profession.

The joy of the family and the church community was necessarily subdued. The NGO that Dennis worked for was interacting with the authorities to try to combat this evil trafficking. Some of the rescued girls were hidden away in country villages because of the fear of the dacoit gangs returning to reclaim them.

With this amazing story ringing in my ears and the confidence that good people were caring for these hospitable people, we posed for another photograph and bid them thanks and goodnight.

I could imagine Basanti singing Psalm 61 1-5 in her distress.

> Hear my cry, O God; listen to my prayer.
> From the ends of the earth I call to you.
> I call as my heart grows faint;
> lead me to the rock that is higher than I.
> For you have been my refuge, a strong tower against the foe.
> I long to dwell in your tent and take refuge
> in the shelter of your wings.

****

(Later I discover it's not a war movie that my Nepali hosts have blazing from their TV sets – it's a direct broadcast of the Gulf War of January 1991!)

Chapter Sixteen

Night Journey to Pokhara

The drum of fire flared. I shivered in the pre-dawn chill. The number thirty-two-bus arrived. 'Pokhara?' I said as instructed. The driver looked down at me and shook his head. Puzzled, I returned to the group of locals around the brazier.

Steam rose through the bright purple, red, and blue stripes of our scarves, muffling our mouths. Our woollen-gloved hands grasped our elbows as we swayed back and forth, waiting for our transport out of Kathmandu.

It was nearly five am and I anxiously watched the number thirty-two-bus. Just then Dennis arrived on his motorbike.

'What are you doing out here? The bus is about to leave. You'd better get on board.' He took my backpack and threw it up to the driver, then helped me up the steps.

(Dennis told me many years later when he was checking this story that the driver had indicated that it was indeed the Pokhara bus. The Nepalis say 'yes' by shaking their heads from side to side and rolling them at the same time. The driver must have wondered why I didn't get on!)

The only seat left was one over the middle wheels, so I travelled with my knees bumping up under my chin. As we drove along, I peered out of the frosted window. Tiny lights sparkled in the galaxy of the Kathmandu valley as women began their chores before the rest of the family awoke. I have seen a symbol for 'woman' in Nepal. It is a woman kneeling with her head on her knees, a man's foot on her back.

I had spent a week in Kathmandu visiting small business enterprises designed to give women freedom from man's mishandling and enslaving. In a backstreet building women gathered each day to spin, dye and weave colourful tote bags and backpacks. Tiny embroidered purses, beanies, and scarves the tourists like to wear were made there. I wore a beautiful necklace finely worked in tiny beads, which was not a tourist bargain but had been paid for in full. Our people carefully ensured that each woman was properly paid for her work. We had no stake in the enterprise other than our desire to see poverty and abuse eliminated from Nepal.

A man sings a Hindi song from the sacred scriptures called *The Beautiful Sura*, which, translated, includes the lines, 'To get work out of your servant, your oxen and your wife, you must give them a good beating.'

I visited community health projects where families were seeing infant mortality rates reduced and malnutrition dealt with. Angie from Melbourne taught village women to write their stories, which had resulted in the transformation of their villages. Wells, piping and electric generators had changed their lives. Around the Pipal trees, schools opened, girls and women together being given the opportunity to rise from under the foot that had traditionally pressed them down. And while all this was going on, the church was growing by the work of the Holy Spirit.

This bus journey would take me to agricultural projects facilitated by NGO's working with and training Nepali men and women. Using hydro electricity, engineering works were developed with Australians and other western nationals working alongside the Nepalis, helping them shape their emerging nation.

This was before the Maoists began their terror campaigns and it was still safe to travel through the back blocks of this beautiful but very impoverished land.

Raylene Pearce

My personal and professional objective was not to possess the grand scenery, or capture the picturesque or panoramic wide-angle views, but to explore the intimate close-ups of many different people — Indian, Nepali, and Expatriate.

To show this: In the cloud behind these girls is the fishtail mountain famous on tourist posters of Nepal called Machhapuchchhre.

After four hours, the bus stopped. The driver yelled something and all the ladies stood up. I followed them off the bus. Each lady, dressed in a sari or long skirt, glided gracefully down the sharp incline of the valley, modestly positioned herself, posing in an elegant straight-backed squat, paused, then giving a tiny little shake, stood upright and proceeded back to the bus. I stood there in my jeans, parka, and gloves with my mouth open, realising that I had missed my chance.

Then came the revelation: No knickers!

Now it was the men's turn, while the ladies refrained from looking out of the windows.

Two hours later, with bladder bulging, I arrived at the Mugling bus station. Here the bus was to turn west towards Pokhara. We stopped for lunch.

Night Journeys

I needed to find a toilet badly. I waddled my way up and down the rows of cafés and souvenir shops. In desperation, I burst into a café and blurted out to the young man making chapattis by the door.

'Toilet!'

Raylene Pearce

He didn't even look up but flipped the egg slice to his left and I tripped towards a door that led to—nowhere.

Amazed, I looked out on an endless image of terraces, like a giant concertina, winding up into the mountains upon mountains of the lower Himalayas.

I noticed a ladder attached to the building, descending into the deep valley. I climbed down and stood sideways, leaning back against the wooden wall of the shop. There was no flat ground to walk upon.

I looked left and right and then saw it. Like a jetty jutting out to sea, a placement of pylons projected a platform out over the valley.

I gingerly crabbed my way until I came to another ladder leading up to the raised platform. I climbed up and shuffled along a narrow horizontal ledge, edging towards a row of waist-high doors.

Opening one, I stepped over to a round hole cut into the wood and looking through, saw pigs scavenging about in the terraced gardens far below.

Enough said.

I was much relieved!

****

I lift up my eyes to the hills - where does my help come from?
(It doesn't come from the hills that's for sure, says author)
My help comes from the LORD,
the maker of heaven and earth.

Psalm 121 v 1 & 2

Chapter Seventeen

India Experiences

Nepal and India opened up my sense of justice and filled my heart with sorrow for oppressed women.

I am fairly naïve, and my innate trust can lead me into trouble. Even when I came to live for the total of ten years in the Middle East, I still gave people the benefit of the doubt.

****

Border Crossing

I walk across the Nepali-India border, a strip of no-man's-land. I present my passport, go through Customs, and pass a row of tiny shops. I'm in the middle of a limestone street, blinding in the midday sun.

Out of one of the darkened booths a tall Indian man grabs my left arm. 'Now you are in India, you wear all bangles on same arm.'

With a mighty swift movement he yanks the glass bangles from my left arm, pulls them across my knobbly knuckles, and shoves them against the other bangles on my right.

I'm completely stunned. The assault on my arms and my wrists is totally unexpected. He completes this transfer of my bangles with a wide grin. Jillian Anderson, my travelling companion, has lived in Africa for many years and is a seasoned traveller with a no-nonsense way about her.

Raylene Pearce

She gives me a disdainful look. 'What are you doing in the middle of the street with that man?'

****

In India I find myself manhandled all the time, from one bus station, train station and border crossing to the next. With wide grins, these misogynistic 'gentlemen' take charge. With a blandishment of a type of courtesy cum flattery, they control me.

I am so naïve that I have been known to follow one gentleman who indicated that he knew where I wanted to go. I had asked him the way to *Allahabad Agricultural College*. He took me through a slum, the size of a small town. On the verge of entering a little shanty, my experienced travelling companion overtook me.

'Do you believe everything you're told?' she asked, taking my arm.

****

While on an Indian train, traveling to Allahabad, I came back to Jillian gagging, 'The toilet is full and overflowing everywhere.'

Holding my hand to my mouth I said, 'What shall we do?'

Jillian stood up, walked into the full size carriage where the single toilet stood in ghastly isolation. She took in the putrid scene, walked over to the toilet, reached up to the chain dangling from a cistern and pulled it.

Out gushed a vast amount of water!

Our fellow passengers didn't understand the function of the chain. What was my excuse?

****

Chapter Eighteen

The Gorakhpur Station Ladies' Waiting Room

We boarded an Indian bus and travelled south to find ourselves waiting for a train on Gorakhpur station. Jillian could sleep anywhere at any time and had already nodded off, propped against the wall on the bench seat in the ladies waiting room.

I cannot sleep properly anywhere or anytime. A young teenage girl who was able to speak some English started to talk to me.

'Hello, my name is Rami.'
'I'm Raylene.' Putting my hands together and bowing my head, I said my only Hindi word.

Raylene Pearce

'*Nameste.*'

'*Nameste,*' returned Rami, her greeting delivered with a bright smile.

There were dozens of women crowded into the ladies waiting room, dressed in *saris*, in the two-piece *shalwa kameez*, wearing woollen shawls with blankets around their shoulders. They watched us with interest.

'Do you have any children?' Rami asked.

I nodded and I took out the photo of my boys. Rami peered into the open faces of Mark-John and James. She passed the photo around and a murmur arose among the ladies. Nodding their heads in approval the women moved closer.

'And where is your husband?'

This is when I come into my own as a cross-cultural communicator. I should also have been a star in silent films.

With my hand on my heart and my eyes cast down, I said in all honesty, 'My husband has divorced me and taken a second wife.'

The whole of the ladies' waiting room erupted in a chorus of connection. I was embraced, kissed, hugged, and stroked. I was swallowed up in the crescendo of women's voices celebrating our shared circumstances; a community of women, cultural differences discarded.

No longer was I just a travelling Australian woman alongside a group of north Indian women—we were all one. A dear lady spread her *sari* out in a space beside her on the hard cement floor, gracefully signing me to enter the *hareem* of her sleeping quarters.

I asked Rami to please explain that I needed to stay awake. My train was expected in the next two hours. I was scared of nodding off through its arrival or, worse still, its departure.

Soon the murmuring subsided and gentle snores wafted around the room.

'Would you like some *chai*, my sister?' Rami whispered.

'Oh, I would like that very much.' I smiled and she took my hand and led me outside to buy *chai*, which was presented in tiny clay cups. As soon as I had finished the sweet tea, Rami took the cup from me

Night Journeys

and smashed it on the platform! I was shocked. I had wanted to keep it and take it home with me. I wanted to be able to say, 'This is the little cup I had *chai* in on Gorakhpur station.' I was denied this souvenir. My clay cup lay smashed among a pile of broken clay cups. I imagined that one day it would be reincarnated as a new clay cup for future customers.

One thing was puzzling me. Why was there no mad rush when the trains arrived? Not one of my ladies moved. Not one of the multitudes waiting on the platforms moved either.

At three in the morning I meandered among the thousands of circles of sleeping families, their feet warming up against the little kerosene stoves making daisy patterns on the huge platforms. I stood amidst the huge panorama of sleeping bodies and suddenly realised that I was standing in the middle of a bedroom. The biggest bedroom in the world!

These people had not come to catch trains. This was their cover for the night. This is where they went every night. Thousands of sleeping families huddled around their little cookers. Eight rows of platforms filled with human beings going nowhere.

And what about my sisters in the ladies' waiting room?

Along with all the other homeless, they were manhandled off the streets of Gorakhpur every night. My new friends were the ones without families who gather around their little kerosene stoves. In the ladies waiting room, built in another era for travelling English ladies of the Raj, the divorced, the widowed and the orphaned had gathered.

I was honoured to be in such special company. I was the same, but completely different. I had the wealth and freedom to make choices — I could move on. These women had nowhere to go. Once cast off through being divorced, deserted or widowed, there was no way back to the family that had paid the dowry to have them married off. There were only the streets, the begging bowl or temple prostitution available to them.

Raylene Pearce

In the past, *sati* would have been their fate—to be covered in ghee and burned on their husband's funeral pyre. At least that got rid of the widow problem. Now they cluttered the streets and the stations. Here I had been welcomed to share a sari-covered piece of cement.

As I was absorbing the horror of the situation, Jillian, who had left the waiting room unnoticed some time before, came back from the stationmaster whispering that our train had derailed. She had made arrangements to have our tickets refunded and we were to take a rickshaw to the bus station. She grabbed her belongings and beckoned me to follow.

With a last look at the company of discarded women, and after a long hug from Rami, I silently made my way out of the Ladies' Waiting Room on Gorakhpur Station to continue our journey to Delhi.

****

A father to the fatherless, a defender of widows,
is God in His holy dwelling.
God sets the lonely in families,
He leads out the prisoners with singing.

Psalm 68 v 5, 6

Chapter Nineteen

Night Journey to Delhi

The early morning mist whirled like white-robed dervishes. We followed our backpacks into the flimsy rickshaw.

Our driver straddled the bike, his head swathed in coiling cheesecloth, his summer-weight clothing covered in a thick woollen shawl. Off we bumped into nothingness. We wobbled along the moonscape of northern India in the heartland of Uttar Pradesh, hoping to be deposited at a bus station.

From out of the dense smog oxen and carts would suddenly materialise, forcing our legs to brace against the front of the swaying vehicle. With our beanies pulled down over eyebrows and ears, our scarves wrapped around mouths and necks, and our gloved hands desperately holding onto the sides of the rickshaw, we squinted into the venomous vapour, thinking:

'We can disappear and no one will know where we are.
'We can get swallowed up in this muck.
'Maybe the stationmaster has noted which driver has taken us out.
'Maybe he hasn't.'

Finally, our driver delivered us to a wavering amber light, softly illuminating the ethereal shroud of the bus station. An oblong shape presented itself and we got in. We smothered ourselves in everything we could find in our backpacks to shield against the cold. We huddled, our knees pressed into our chests, concerned our feet would fall off with frostbite if we let them stray, unprotected, beneath the seat.

Suddenly, a man loomed above me, yelled something, grabbed my arms, and pulled me off the bus.

Raylene Pearce

Jillian followed, yelling, 'Stop it! You can't just do that!'

Ignoring her completely, the man reached in, seized our backpacks, and threw them off with us.

'Delhi—this one,' called another man, who immediately took our packs and tossed them on the roof of a nearby bus. He pushed us up the steps. The bus was packed with humans and animals and was about to move off. We crawled into a narrow front seat.

To our amazement the bus didn't have a windscreen! The driver was wrapped in multiple layers of clothing and woollen gloves. A thick turban wound around his head and mouth made him look like the abominable snowman. He drove at breakneck speed, refuting that analogy. We prayed up a regiment of guardian angels as the snowman narrowly missed all oncoming traffic.

Apparitions of donkeys, bell-ringing monks, sacred cows, family-covered pushbikes, and what looked like walking trees appeared as passing ghosts.

There was nowhere to put our legs. Our seat was jammed up against the partition by the door and we tried sitting sideways as our knees kept colliding with the livestock in the aisle. Our bus was filled with howling banshees, whirling dervishes, and frozen ears.

Being manhandled was a way of life for the women of Nepal and India. The road from Kathmandu to Delhi was no place for wimpy women.

This night journey was to lead us to projects in New Delhi. Families built shanties beside the giant skyscrapers they erected for the banking companies of the world. Men dangled like insects from bamboo scaffolding. Women carried bricks and mortar on their backs every day, seven days a week. Later those without a shanty, would warm themselves against the northern-Indian winter night chill around their kerosene stoves at the nearest railway station.

In the transformed slums we were welcomed into homes, resurrected from building site scrap. The Project facilitated covered drains and even electric light to make life safer and more convenient. We saw

93

school children reciting their lessons and women bent happily over sewing machines. No sweat shops here, but opportunities to come out of poverty. To make clothes for their families and extra to sell in the shop, opened especially for the artisans of the Project.

In a one-room dwelling, a highly polished dung floor, reflected a wife proudly displaying her shiny plates and pans on a shelf attached to the cow dung stuccoed wall.

She offered us chai from a well-scrubbed kettle.

****

The poor will see and be glad—
you who seek God, may your hearts live!
The LORD hears the needy
and does not despise his captive people.

Psalm 69 v 32 & 33

Chapter Twenty

Flying Solo
Adelaide to Cyprus
(1994 – 1999)

Back in June 1994 there were sixty people to see me off at Adelaide airport. I felt so calm. Here I was leaving everyone I had loved, some for all my life. Not for a six weeks holiday but for two and a half years. I was travelling overseas for the first time on my own. The Great Adventure had begun. I was beginning a new life.

Since 1990 after being recruited by an Egyptian woman working in media I had been preparing for this day. After completing various writing courses at the Adelaide TAFE I completed subjects from the *Australian College of Divinity* in Canberra and through the *Bible College of South Australia*. I was working full time and taking one subject each semester. New Testament, Old Testament, Missions, History of Mission, Cross Cultural Communication, Other Religions: Islam etc. During that time I was a student, a Mission Representative, and a member of the BCSA Council.

At the airport I remember speaking to my friends and each member of my family until the last minutes came. I held onto Mark-John and kissed both him and Alison. I then turned to my younger son James. That's when I lost it. I clung to him, bawling into his shoulder, the poor boy embarrassed by his, usually, reasonably calm mother.

The plane was due to leave at seven pm on this cool Thursday evening. But I was still at the terminal clinging to James. I remember a ground staff member trying to get me to let go, anxious that I get

Night Journeys

onto the waiting plane. I couldn't believe I was acting like this! Many of my missionary colleagues were watching me and various family members were getting a bit teary. Eventually I turned, gathered my belongings, and without looking back walked heavy-legged towards the aircraft.

The plan was that I would fly to Melbourne and transfer to an international flight later that night. Some Melbourne colleagues had said they would meet me to fill in the time till I caught a Gulf Air flight to Singapore at ten pm. I was due for a brief stop there and in Bahrain. Then I would be met at Larnaca International Airport on the island of Cyprus the following day. *The Company* colleagues would convey me to Nicosia, my new home. Such are the plans of mice and women. How many things can go wrong for someone on her first lone flight journeying into the night?

I cried all the way to Melbourne, making myself vomit and feeling thoroughly ashamed. As the plane taxied in I pulled myself together. I entered the airport to be greeted by a dozen Melbourne colleagues lead by Berys, the Personnel Director, of *The Company* (Australia).

There was one woman called Heather Morley whom I had only met a few months before. At ten pm they announced that the connecting flight was delayed. It hadn't even left Sydney!

I sent the others off home but Heather said, 'I will not leave you till you walk through those doors,' indicating the large dull steel doors leading to the departure lounge.

At eleven pm Gulf Air announced that the flight would not arrive at all that night. The passengers would need to return to the airport the following day. There were no rooms available at the airport hotel, but they would give us each a taxi voucher.

Heather insisted that I spend the night at her home. The time it took to drive across Melbourne to get to Heather's place in Dandenong took twice as long as the flight from Adelaide to Melbourne.

The next morning I rang Mark-John to tell him, 'No, I'm not ringing from Singapore but from Melbourne.' And I told him what happened.

Raylene Pearce

'If Heather had not stayed with me I would have had to sit all night at Melbourne airport.'
We used the taxi voucher and arrived at the airport at ten am. Still, the Sydney plane could not leave because of high winds. Once again, Heather and I sat it out.

****

After moving out of my home, dividing furniture and belongings among friends and relatives, moving in with James, packing and sending my unaccompanied luggage ahead, packing for the trip, eating goodbye-dinners, handing over the office to my successor and leaving my friends and family, nothing would faze me on the trip.
Or so I thought.
Eventually at two-thirty pm on Friday we took off. My non-smoking seat bunged up against the toilets, two rows from the intense smokers who happily shared their cancerous smog all the way to Singapore. In Singapore I was able to change my seat to one further away from the smokers.
Not sleeping a wink, I was greeted with the news that because the plane was so late arriving in Bahrain, we had missed our connecting flight. We were to be put up at the Gulf Hotel.
There I was in the lap of luxury: a glam bathroom with white fluffy towels. I indulged myself and had two bubble baths, free meals, and an opportunity to observe the ways of travelling Cypriots who were none too pleased at the ongoing delays.
On the following day, Saturday at five-thirty pm, we sat in the Bahrain departure lounge waiting to be herded like stunned cattle onto the airport bus. Then came the announcement that seven of us could not fit on the plane.
Cyprus Airways had sent a much smaller plane and I was in the group that was told that they would have to stay the whole weekend in Bahrain. There were no more flights to Cyprus till Monday. This did

Night Journeys

not suit an Australian/Greek archaeologist who was going to work on a dig in the centre of Cyprus. Angela had a huge wooden box of archaeological specimens with her. She demanded that she be let on the plane and that the box go with her.

After a sustained ruckus, the airline decided to let us all on the plane without our luggage! Angela insisted on her wooden crate going with her. We were jammed three people to two seats – guess who had to perch in the middle of two seats? The specimen box filled the aisle. The hour journey, though crowded, was uneventful.

I was now arriving in Cyprus two days late!

****

For this reason I kneel before the Father,
from whom his whole family in heaven and on earth derives its name.
I pray that out of his glorious riches he may strengthen you with power through his spirit in your inner being,
so that Christ may dwell in your hearts through faith.
And I pray that you, being rooted and established in love,
may have power, together with all the saints,
to grasp how wide and long and high and deep
is the love of Christ,
and to know his love that surpasses knowledge
– that you may be filled to the measure of all the fullness of God.

Ephesians 3 v 14 – 19

Part Four

Cyprus

Chapter Twenty One

Island in the Sun (June 1994)

Without any luggage, I was one of the first to walk into the smoke-filled, people-crushed tin shed to find no one there to meet me. I sat and watched effusive Cypriots embracing and greeting each other in huge voices, their emotions overflowing. Still no one arrived for me. I rang the various phone numbers I had been given but no one was answering.

I had presumed that the airline would answer any queries from my new colleagues regarding my expected time of arrival. Apparently only incorrect information was offered. So I sat there from nine pm until the airport started to empty and only Cyprus Airways Staff was left. I asked what I should do.

An angel called Anthony Christodoulos said, 'You can be our representative from Australia! You must come in our bus to Nicosia. We will put you up in the Excelsior Hotel. In the morning you will be able to contact your friends.'

He was so friendly and no one objected. An hour later we arrived at a pitch-black block of empty space where the staff had left their cars.

Anthony invited me into his car. 'I will take you to the Excelsior. You will like it there.'

I remember getting into the passenger seat, clutching my hand luggage and wondering if I'd ever be seen again. I wasn't afraid. Instead of fear there was just a feeling of otherworldliness. And now with no one to meet me, I was at the mercy of a man whose name in English meant 'slave of Christ'. He was true to his name and deposited me at the Excelsior Hotel safely and graciously.

Night Journeys

So there I was, sitting up in bed in another hotel. I still couldn't get anyone to answer phones in Nicosia. Later I found out that they were all out at the movies. That made it all right. If they had been anywhere else I would have been most put out! But the movies - that's a good excuse. I would be making use of the many cinemas in Nicosia before the year was out.

At twelve thirty in the morning I called Berys at the Melbourne office. Berys told me that two of my new colleagues, Andrew and Muriel, who were returning from a wedding in Limassol, had rung from the airport saying that they were there to meet me. They had been told I was arriving on Jordanian Airlines. About the time I was being the Australian Representative for Cyprus Airlines on the staff bus hurtling along the road to Nicosia, they were asking at the Jordanian airline counter as to why I wasn't on board. Then Berys rang from Australia and told them I was at the Excelsior Hotel in Nicosia. They continued home. I stayed the night in the hotel.

The phone bills cost almost as much as the airfare!

The next morning I was picked up by one of the movie goers, Margaret, and taken to church. It was a great delight for me that on my first day in Nicosia I was worshipping the Lord with work mates. I had lunch with Alex and Deirdre and taken to the flat in Lykavitos which became my home for the next two years.

Some days later my luggage arrived with clothes and other necessities. Later still, my unaccompanied luggage came. Hurrah!

Life on the island of Cyprus as the Personnel Director of a media organisation, and five years of international and Middle Eastern travel was about to begin.

****

Raylene Pearce

For it is by grace you have been saved, through faith -
and this not from yourselves,
it is the gift of God -
not by works, so that no one can boast.

For we are God's workmanship,
created in Christ Jesus
to do good works,
which God prepared in advance
for us to do.

Paul's letter to the Ephesians 2: 8 -10

Chapter Twenty Two

Divided Life
(1994 – 1999)

Here I am walking beside the broken brickwork, the dividing wall that has separated southern and northern Nicosia and the whole of Cyprus since 1964. Because of the unrest, the Turkish Cypriots left the south and retreated to enclaves of safety in the north. Greeks living in the north were forced out of their homes and moved south. Since 1974 the United Nations have been keeping peace between the fractured communities. No Man's Land extends for 200 kms across Cyprus.

Imagine a giant wheel with lines connecting at the hub. On the edge of the wheel imagine high ancient walls with huge ramparts stretching over the moat and eleven bastions shaped like onion heads. Bastions are huge gated areas with room for hundreds of soldiers to gather to repeal an attack. They are used now for art galleries and concert halls – great atmosphere.

Imagine another line, this time through the centre. This is the *Green Line*. I lived in the southern side of the circle, the Greek Cypriot side. The other half of the wheel to the north is occupied by Turkey.

In 1489 the city of Nicosia was built by the Venetians. But in 1570 the Turks overran the walls and created two communities. The trauma of that and subsequent invasions and hostilities continued to feed the hatred and separation between the Greek and Turkish Cypriots to this day.

I'm with Carla, a Canadian, and Margaret, an Englishwoman, both colleagues. This is my first look at the wall, festooned on top with barbed wire, with graffiti decorating the cement sides. It is ten o'clock on a warm July night not long after I arrive in Cyprus. Thick darkness cloaks us as smoke from bush fires hover overhead. No light except for the weak torch dying in Carla's hand. In the heart of the round city the stars are extinct.

Without warning, an Argentinian soldier, rifle pointed at us, his U.N. powder blue beret perched above a sweet face like a ten year old playing 'commando', stepped out of the darkness. We knew he was Argentinian because it was this country's turn to take on the task of maintaining the peace.

'Turn around and go back the way you came.' He barked.

'Er sorry, we didn't think we had gone this far' was the lame excuse uttered by Carla, who was destined to face much graver obstacles in the future. She was due to leave for Afghanistan the following month, just as the Taliban were taking charge.

With much bowing and scraping the three of us shuffled back the way we came. The muggy air celebrated the beginning of holidays. Barbecued chicken, souvlaki, yiros and onions wafted from the open front doors of homes that backed onto the forbidden area. The war was over, but now the war raged in the hearts of the old folk who couldn't forgive while their island remained divided. There is no resolution when land and honour is at stake.

Back into the half of the city freely available to us we checked out the open doors of the houses, living rooms leading directly into the street. The passageways might lead into the inner courtyard where perhaps a fountain flowed and roses grew like something out of *The Thousand and One Nights*. Over the doorways wrought iron scrolls like curly crowns proclaimed the year the house was built – 1912, 1921, 1933. Most doors hinted of a time when they were bright and beautiful, but now the paint was dull and peeling, crying out for restoration.

The problem with the upkeep was that many of these homes belonged to Turkish Cypriots who had been forced to leave the south and move north and no one could claim them – not while the island remained divided.

Two great Turkish flags hacked out of the hillside painted bright red and white remind the Greek Cypriots of the invasion. These two huge flags can be seen from most areas of the Greek side of the city. The Turkish Cypriots expect no one looking from the Greek side will ever forget the Turks have as much right as the Greeks to be there.

Forget! That's something they will never do. It is the main topic of conversation on everyone's lips. Commencing in the morning, with the old men sitting in twos at cafe tables on the pavements, their Cypriot coffee and glass of water at their elbows, the backgammon board between them. One opens the newspaper and the politics start.

Their wives are busy getting the grandchildren off to school. The grandchildren's parents, probably professionals who live in their own apartment, bring the children to either grandparent so that they can start work early. The landlords in my first flat were both dentists. Louisa never learned to cook and her mother virtually cared for the two boys. When I was invited to dinner they would always get take-a-way.

At the end of the school day the children would do their homework at Grandma's and eat a meal before the siesta from 2-4pm. Businesses and shops would open again and close at 7pm. Much later, about 10pm, families would eat dinner together, children, parents, and other relatives from either side of the family talking about the latest infringement by Turkey on their land.

I found Greek Cypriots hospitable. When I ate at one of the office girl's home in her village, we would all sit out in the backyard with the grafted lemon and orange tree sheltering us from the afternoon heat. Every now and then I would flash a look of consternation in the direction of Athena across the table.

She would call out to me, 'Don't worry, Raylene, they aren't arguing. They always talk this loud.'

A North American woman I knew, married to a Cypriot, said, 'Because there are so many people of different generations in one house you have to speak very loudly, so no one thinks that they are being talked about behind their back.' Other Cypriots deny this, but I have seen and heard a grandfather yelling, like a crazed person, at a little boy about four years old while he's sitting on grandfather's knee.

I did ask Athena if Cypriots had a collective kind of deafness!

I've been lost in Nicosia many times. I found it hard to negotiate narrow streets honing inwards like spokes in half a wheel. Coming from Adelaide with its straight streets and only one called Diagonal Road was no training ground for the half circles and diagonals criss-crossing Nicosia (*Lefcosia*), the capital city of Cyprus.

I wasn't the only one getting lost in the rabbit warren of Nicosia. Taxi drivers didn't have a clue. An all-night taxi company set up shop in the empty block next to my building. Everyone who knows me knows I have trouble sleeping in the best of circumstances. I couldn't sleep in the front room of the first floor flat because a huge ALL NIGHT TAXI fluorescent lit sign penetrated the room and made sleeping on hot nights impossible. Moving to the back room where the window looked out onto the pre-fab office was impossible as well. A man sat at a table, in a white plastic chair, yelling at the top of his voice into a microphone like there was no wireless connection between him and the lost drivers.

On the other side of the vacant lot (I say vacant because the taxi company had illegally taken it over) was a Maternity Hospital. They took the taxi company to court and won. In the best of all possible worlds the taxi company would have been moved on. But someone knew someone and an exchange of something permitted the taxi company to stay. I finally moved to another flat. I couldn't wait for the Cypriot courts to get their act together. I guess the new mothers moved out as soon as possible, but it would have been hard on the staff.

But living in Lykovitos, Nicosia, I did enjoy the balcony. It was a favourite place for visitors to sit and chat with me. In the second year I lived there Heather Morley came to visit. Heather was the friend who took me home to Dandenong, when the Gulf Air plane never arrived

Night Journeys

to take me to Cyprus. One afternoon we were sitting chatting in our summer clothes when all of a sudden the sky opened and pelted us with hail! We had been swimming at Aphrodite's rocks that morning.

Once there was a huge ruckus with sirens screaming on and on. I went onto the balcony expecting to see the neighbours doing the same. No one showed. I stood there nonplussed as the sirens continued to flood the air. I retreated into the flat and turned on the radio but was none the wiser – it was *'all Greek'* to me!

To this day I don't know what that was all about. There is a real disadvantage of not knowing what is happening around you when you don't have the language. This was my lot on many occasions. While on Cyprus I was learning Arabic, as that was the heart language of the people I had come to serve.

Early one morning, at 3.47 exactly, an explosion resonated down my street. I raced onto the balcony and again no one else appeared. The morning's news said that at 3.47am the Russian mafia blew up a nightclub owner when he started his car. Next time it happened I didn't bother to get up, but checked the time.

'*What we are saying, is give peace a chance.*'

Once more I'm out on my balcony. I could hear this song wafting across the old city to my right. An historic meeting was taking place. Greek Cypriot young people had gathered to meet with Turkish Cypriot youth on the soccer pitch beside no man's land.

I heard the following day that this first time event of its kind went very well. Young people linked arms and danced and sang songs they all knew and ate food they were all familiar with. They found so much in common they were amazed. Separated by a dividing city wall, each group had grown up being taught to hate the other. My friend Nicki's little girl Irina marched at Kindy and sang 'Kill a Turk, kill a Turk' to keep the children in step! In step with their grandparents whose major pass-time was the 'The Turkish Problem'.

After a while I went inside and turned on the local TV channel. It showed a rubbish bin on fire in Elethera Square, nowhere near where the young people were. A few old people gathered on one side of the square. The following morning, BBC World Service reported, 'The worst riots in Cyprus history....blah, blah, blah...' That bin on fire looked like a building, flames filling the screen.

Such is life on a divided island with a divided people.

****

Jesus said:
'If a kingdom is divided against itself,
that kingdom cannot stand.
If a house is divided against itself, that house cannot stand.'

Mark 3 v 24, 25

Chapter Twenty Three

Methuselah and Me (1997)

The day after I returned from my first Home Assignment I was due for dinner at a friend's place. Dressed in an apricot skirt and white shirt I looked spick and span. I went downstairs to greet Methuselah.

Athena had been flat sitting for me but I found out later that she was too ashamed of Methuselah to keep him charged up! All I asked her to do was take him out every week for a run around the neighbourhood. That was the problem. Too many people in the neighbourhood knew her. Seeing her driving the multi-coloured bluish 1974 Toyota Corolla station wagon would set all the tongues wagging.

The locals would never have appreciated that Methuselah had had a very colourful history. He had been driven overland over twenty years before from Scotland to England and on the ferry to France. He had gone by road all through Europe with a group of hippies. After checking out all the Asian sights, he arrived in Cyprus via Egypt by barge. He had gone over a cliff once, which would have been the end of most modern cars. He was restored over and over the years by various guys happy to be up to their armpits in grease.

International volunteers working on the Island owned him from time to time. I met a man in Lebanon who was responsible for giving Methuselah a heart transplant. I had inherited him from an Australian girl working with an NGO, for four hundred Cyprus pounds, about one thousand Australian dollars at the time. At the end of my stay on Cyprus I gave him to my Norwegian friend Helga. One day her husband apparently took him on a journey from which he did not return - Methuselah, not the husband.

Raylene Pearce

I was sad to hear it.

Methuselah lived in a carport under the flats. This day he refused to start. I called the Road Assist people and they charged the battery and suggested I take him for a long drive to keep up the charge. Out on the highway to Larnaca the back tyre blew and I swerved to a halt on the side of the road.

I got out and sat in the passenger side because the cars racing along the freeway sort of un-nerved me. As I sat there wondering what to do a policeman knocked on the window. I got out and showed him the tyre, asking for his help. He gave me a long look and walked around the car. He spoke on his walkie-talkie and continued his close examination of Methuselah.

'Who owns this car?'

'I do.'

'Who drives this car?'

'I do.'

'Why are you sitting in the passenger seat?'

'Scared of the fast cars whizzing by.'

He walked once more around me and came back and peered into my face. He looked me up and down taking in my spotless apricot skirt and white blouse.

He said, 'Why don't you get rid of it?'

Horrified, I said, 'No way. This is my car,' and with shameful mumbling, 'I can't afford another,' I asked him again if he could call the Road Assist people. Apparently he had done that earlier.

With a big sigh my policeman asked for my papers and then tried to get the wheel off. After about thirty minutes the Road Assist people turned up and they couldn't get the wheel off either. I was dropped off home, sitting high in the front of the tow truck. Methuselah, travelling behind, looked very sorry for himself. He spent the night at the Garage.

Methuselah had several features that made him special. To open the back door all you had to do was stick your thumb in the hole where the lock usually is on other cars, and the door would spring open. Also, when

Night Journeys

people rode with me and they appeared to be a bit anxious, I'd suggest they look at another hole, this time in the floor beside the gear stick, about the size of an orange. As they peered into it they could check out the road whizzing by. This was supposed to make people feel secure.

Methuselah was very misunderstood. My boss forbade me to pick up VIP's from the airport in him. I was puzzled. My boss told me to take a taxi – an unnecessary expense to our organisation, I thought. But picking up friends offered much mirth, especially when I took them into the old city, driving fairly fast down narrow lanes and later backing into my carport narrowly missing a sturdy cement column. A cup of tea usually worked to bring the colour back into their faces.

Another time I had Methuselah filled up with food etc for a staff camp on Troodos in the mountains above Nicosia. I was driving alone on a near empty road when a policeman on a motorcycle came up alongside me and motioned me to stop.

I did so and got out of my heavily laden car.

'Do you know how fast you were going?'

'No, no, I don't know. I'm alone on the road.'

I wasn't going to tell him that one of the other features of Methuselah's was that the speedo didn't work. I usually gauged how fast I was going on the highway by how many cars I overtook.

He shook his head and asked me, 'Could I see your driver's license please?'

'Oh yes,' I said as I shuffled the dusty papers in the glove box. 'Here it is.'

I presented him with the folded sheet.

He opened it. 'This license is out of date.'

'Is it?' I asked. 'Oh dear, I've been off island and haven't checked.'

A sort of hopeful look gathered on my face.

'Can I see the registration? And while you are there, could I see your insurance papers too?'

They were in as bad a state as my other papers. At least my passport was OK.... I hoped.

Raylene Pearce

'Where are you going?' he asked.

'I'm heading for the Troodos Camp Site. See,' indicating the cartons of groceries, loaves of bread, drinks, fold-up chairs. 'My car is filled with food for the campers.'

Nod, nod, nervous smile.

'Off you go, then, and make sure you get all your papers renewed on Monday.' (It was Friday afternoon.)

I was very ebullient, 'Thank you officer.'

Needless to say, I drove a bit slowly until another car came along. I put my impatient foot to the pedal, glancing at the road beneath as I made my way upwards towards the mountains. It's so reassuring to have that hole in the floor beside the gear stick.

You know just where you are!

And the LORD also knows.

****

You discern my going out and my lying down;
you are familiar with all my ways.

Psalm 139 v 3

Chapter Twenty-Four

Never go North

Knowing where you are and whether you are supposed to be there can be a problem. On another occasion a group of work colleagues and a woman holidaying from Greece, a friend of one of our International Office staff, went over to the 'other side'. It was during Heather's visit.

We passed through the Ledra Palace checkpoint where our passports were checked. The policeman frowned and nodded toward the propaganda on walls and posters like 'Do not spend your money in Northern Cyprus' and 'Do not support the invaders.' We were aware that our Greek Cypriot friends could not do this, so when we went 'over' we didn't tell them.

Then we went through the UN buffer zone, or 'no man's land', with the burned out, pockmarked ruins of that which was once central Nicosia. This is a very surreal place reminiscent of apocalyptic movies we had all seen. At the Turkish Cypriot checkpoint police scrutinised our passports, clicked away at a computer terminal and sent us on our way through the northern side of Nicosia.

We stopped off at the Cathedral of Santa Sophia. I was interested in a crusader tomb, so took a photo. I was never to see the image I had taken; to my disgust found I had run out of film. I relaxed when Heather offered to copy her photos for me. She had two cameras, one of which looked like a packet of cough-lozenges, was disposable, and shot wide-angle images.

After leaving the city we drove upwards to the Byzantine castle of St Hilarian built in the 10th century and dismantled in 1489 by one of Cyprus' many invaders, the Venetians. After climbing the rocky outcrops supporting the ruins we returned to the car, driving through villages and taking photographs.

At one of these we got out and stretched our legs. The place seemed deserted but the Greek woman took some photos anyway. We had been photographing the scenes in the background where a recent bush fire had burnt out a large portion of the hills. (We had watched it burn a week ago. Many Greek Cypriots were hysterical because the fire was in the area of the homes they had to leave in 1974 when the island was divided.)

We continued to the east coast and swam at Salamis where Paul and Barnabas had landed two millennia before. Inland from the long shallow beach, we waded in long grass, treading on priceless mosaics. Yes, priceless mosaics! We sat on and posed by huge Roman statues in an ancient gymnasium and amphitheatre. Nowhere did we see any policing of these amazing ruins.

After lunch in a café on the harbour of Kyrenia we watched men and boys diving off the harbour wall in their underpants. This seemed to be a lunchtime activity. We had hoped to visit the huge Byzantine/Lusignan/Venetian/British castle jutting into the harbour, but it was closed. The wide corniche was lined with fish cafés and tiny tourist shops. Flaky pastel-coloured apartments filled in the gaps and fishing boats lined up secured to the harbour wall. It reminded me of the images that jigsaw puzzlers love to lean over, spending hours to re-create such a scene.

As the afternoon wore on, we headed back to the Turkish checkpoint, snapping photos and appreciating the beautiful scenery as we went. We had to be back by 5.30pm as the border closed then. After arriving at the border crossing, it was quickly apparent that something wasn't right. We were told as we climbed out of our vehicle to hand over our cameras.

I complained. 'I have only taken one photo - the crusader tomb in the Cathedral of Santa Sophia. Then I ran out of film. I was very disappointed.'

The police weren't interested in my disappointment, and took my film anyway. I whispered to Heather to only take her proper camera out and leave the one that looked like a packet of cough lollies in her beach bag. Although our things were searched this camera wasn't recognised. We still have the wide-angle shots of Kyrenia harbour and the Roman ruins at Salamis.

After some time of questioning, it appeared that our Greek lady's husband came from the village she photographed.

Photographing these places was absolutely forbidden. Someone had noticed her taking photos of the ghost town, took the car's number plate, and reported us. On both sides there was shame in allowing these villages to fall into decay. Letting it be known how bad the deserted villages were, was taboo.

After we returned I made a point of walking to the checkpoint once a week, asking for my photos back. The police would have viewed the Filipino girls in swimsuits sitting on the beach eating huge slices of watermelon. Those girls kept asking me for copies because it was the day of their baptism in the Mediterranean Sea. And I kept going back to the checkpoint. My photos had nothing to do with Cyprus politics, but I think the police enjoyed having them around!

Some of the excuses were, 'The Commandant is at lunch; not at work today; hasn't returned from a meeting; isn't here.' He was even sick on one occasion.

I gave up.

****

> Therefore, since through God's mercy
> we have this ministry,
> we do not lose heart.
> For we do not preach ourselves,
> but Jesus Christ as Lord.
>
> 2 Corinthians 4 v 1, 5, 6

Chapter Twenty Five

Blacklisted

About a year later, James, my younger son, came to stay with me. While we were waiting for Mark-John and Alison, my first-born and daughter-in-law, to arrive on the island, I took him for a drive in Northern Cyprus. We went through the usual checkpoints and headed north towards Kyrenia, hoping that this time the castle on the harbour would be open.

After a while James said, 'Mum, there's a man in a car waving at you.'

I looked across and, sure enough, there was a man in a little brown car waving at me. We got to some red lights.

He jumped out of his car and said, 'Are you Mrs Stephens?'

'Yes I am.'

'Turn back. Go back to where you came from.'

I was astounded. 'But we've only just got here.'

'Turn around.'

'I want to show my son your lovely country.'

'Go.'

This time his face looked darkly menacing and he was pointing south.

'But why?'

'You are forbidden. Go back! I will follow you.'

There were one or two cars lined up behind us, so when another green light showed I turned right and turned again to go back to where I came from.

My escort followed. Trouble is, going south doesn't necessarily mean that you will end up where you were supposed to be. I've been lost many times in the south side of the round city and driving in the north was just as complex.

'I wonder,' I mused, 'I wonder if they have a record of my previous visit?'

'I think you're blacklisted, Mum. Nothing would surprise me,' said my son, who arrived in the cold of winter without any warm clothes. For the duration of his visit he wore my boss's brown leather jacket.

Then I got lost. I thought it was fairly straight. But when you enter a round city every road veers offside and before you know it – you're lost. My little man in the little brown car was apparently beeping his horn, which is a common sound in this part of the world, and I took no notice. When he started flashing his lights I thought perhaps I should stop.

'I'm lost,' my face full of confusion looking up into his.

His narrowed eyes glared at me.

'I come in front. You follow me!'

As if I had deliberately set out to be lost!

The little motorcade travelled at some speed (I didn't know how fast of course) but James noticed the difference.

'I think he wants to get rid of you, Mum.'

'At least he's got something to tell his wife when he gets home. Something other than the Greek problem.'

We entered the Turkish Check Point to shouts and arms waving.

My elusive Commandant advanced with hands on hips.

'Why are you here? You are forbidden!'

'I didn't know,' was my forlorn reply.

I was escorted to the office and we looked up at a row of TV consuls. On one of them was my name and in the left upper corner was a small black box.

'See, you are forbidden.'

'I'm amazed. I wanted to take my son....'

'No more! We let you off this time but if you come again there will be consequences.'

I was going to ask him if I could have my photos back as the Filipino girls were still asking for them. They looked so cute in their bathing costumes.

I decided against it.

My primary and heart-felt work was off-island and that's where my story continued.

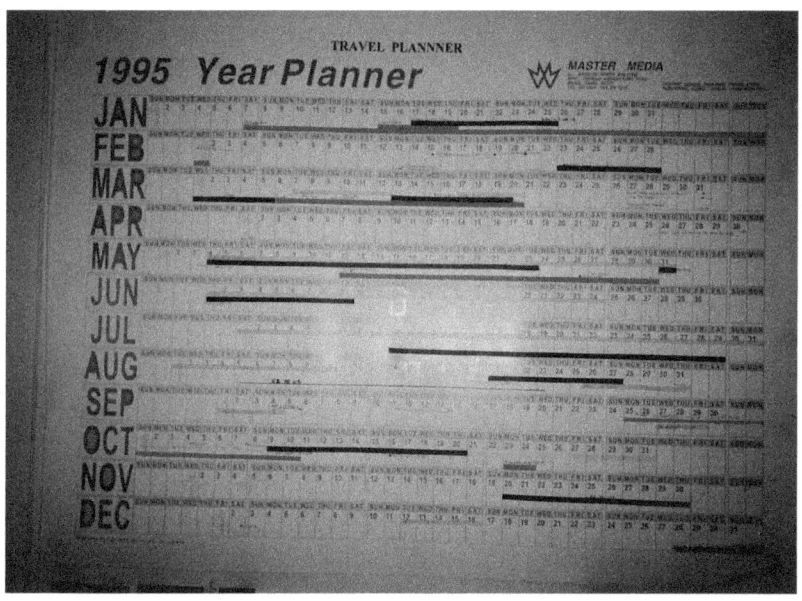

The dark blue lines indicate the trips I took off Island

****

Night Journeys

He will not let your foot slip -
he who watches over you will not slumber;
indeed, he who watches over Israel
will neither slumber nor sleep.

The LORD watches over you -
the LORD is your shade at
your right hand;
the sun will not harm you by day
nor the moon by night.

The LORD will keep you from all harm -
he will watch over your life;
the LORD will watch over your coming and going
both now and forevermore.

Psalm 121: 3 - 8

Part Five

Off Island

Chapter Twenty Six

Connections, Connections, Connections
Turkey Anyone? (1990's)

Cyprus is central to many locations, and Turkey is only a short flight away if you are a sea gull. Because of the divided Island we are not allowed to fly over the north. We have to fly to Athens and then onto Turkey, a confusing flight path for any self respecting seagull.

I made several trips to colleagues, to check their mental, physical, and spiritual health. Issues of work concerns and their need for more volunteers were investigated and followed up.

On one trip I attended a conference in Antalya on the south coast where the children swam in the hotel pool and the beach. In the afternoon, after a final swim, we flew from there to Istanbul and the next morning I opened my curtains and gazed out at a wonderland of snow! During the night a transformation had taken place and what had been red tiled rooves and stark black trees embracing the edge of the Bosporus became a Dickens's Christmas card.

I was completing my week visiting this fascinating country where we had families working in literature work. I took great pleasure in this pastoral role, culminating in the gift of the snow. Walking to the *Book House* I couldn't help reverting to a deprived childhood that had never had the joys of soft flaky snow. So I kicked the stuff around and kept scooping it up in my gloved hands. Almost got smacked in the face by a flying snowball in the main street!

Night Journeys

The next day I had to leave. The little taxi man looked back at me with a perplexed look. Was it the ninth time or the tenth time that he had to stop because of his non-heated windscreen and the faulty wipers? Or was it the eleventh time that he had to draw onto the side of the road and scrape the snow and ice off the windscreen?

I gave him what I hoped was a reassuring smile and indicated that I would continue to pray. He'd wipe one side of the windscreen and as he wiped the other, the first side froze over! It got worse when we left the huge snow cloud and encountered the sun, which blinded him through the crystallised glass.

He was not alone. All along the route to the airport were little taxis parked by the side of the road, their drivers frantically scraping their windscreens. Eventually we got to the airport with just enough time to check in.

I had to walk out on to the tarmac, snow covered and slippery, then find my luggage piled up near the back of the waiting plane. Once found, it was loaded on. It was rather nerve-wracking as not only was the ground slippery but I had to contend with a strong wind.

God is good. He gives me adventures while I do my pastoral work and he gives me surprises too.

****

She had written from Adelaide before she took off for her European holiday with her friend Jude. They were planning a visit to Cairo, so I sent her a list of do's and don'ts while travelling in a male dominated Muslim country. I had to go to Turkey and we never got to see each other.

Then high in the sky between Istanbul and Athens we met! I hadn't seen Gillian Murdoch for years, but recognised her when I boarded the plane.

After the plane took off I went back to her seat, leant over her travelling companion and said 'Miss Murdoch I presume?'

Raylene Pearce

After squeals of delight, she handed me the postcard she was writing. It said: Dear Raylene .... She planned to post it once they had landed in Athens. It was from Pompeii, and she was going to write on it saying what a wonderful time they were having in Italy and regrettably they were not going to have the time to visit Egypt (and see me) after Turkey.

How about that? How many people have an experience like that? In mid-air two people meet, who didn't even know that they were in transit in the same area, one of them writing a postcard to the other!

So we continued the flight down the cabin away from the other passengers. Three Aussies talking non-stop, not quite believing they were on the same plane.

I am continually amazed at what God can do. Of all places for a reunion! Especially as they had cancelled their trip to Egypt and didn't know that I had work in the country they were currently visiting. I let their parents, Ian and Glenys, friends and supporters of mine, know about this adventure and how well the girls looked.

And what did that mean? They were totally gorgeous with Botticelli curls branching out in all directions. Must have driven the Italians mad! They were having a great time dodging amorous advances in Italy and Turkey. I guess having to face the Egyptian male gaze, and more, would be too much for any girl - even our modern young things.

****

O LORD you have searched me and you know me.
You know when I sit and when I rise;
you perceive my thoughts from afar.
You discern my going out and my lying down;
you are familiar with all my ways.

Psalm 139 v 1, 2

Night Journeys

Lebanon Nights
(March 1996)

West Beirut at night must be one of the weirdest places outside of Bosnia. Stark, broken-in-half high-rise buildings with front rooms completely missing, greeted us as we bumped our way over vanishing roads. On each side, blasted buildings, pockmarked walls, naked windows beckoned the moon to enter. Now and then a yellow light flickered through a jagged hole in a wall, indicating that people were trying to live there. Syrian soldiers living in skeletal shells!

I was surprised to see large posters of the Iranian religious leader, the Ayatollah Khamenei, decorating every street. I guessed Syria, as 'peace keepers' in the aftermath of the 12 years' long Lebanese civil war, wanted to make their allegiance known to both sides of the conflict.

Through numerous checkpoints manned by Syrian soldiers, we swerved from one side of the road to the other to avoid huge potholes or bomb craters. Markus was taking me to the monastery at Jouneith. Markus was also the person who gave my car a heart transplant some years before. He was pleased to hear that Methuselah was going fine, heart beating strong.

We were to travel along the coast where the first ever Arabic Media Convention was to be held. One of the forward planning hopes for this civil-war-recovering country was that through the good use of creative media the infrastructure of the devastation could be repaired. Markus' ministry was in transformation too. He was in the process of moving from printed products to the Internet, and the use of mobile phones to spread the Gospel. Everything was changing.

The following weekend on the road to Damascus, surrounded by snow-clad hills like veiled maidens at a wedding, we drove through the old Druze area. The Druze, an Islamic sect, were overwhelmed during the twelve years of civil war. Their shattered farms spilling into the Bakke Valley were little more than bombed out ruins piled up beside the brand new condominiums.

Our *Company* had people there who were trying to connect through innovative farming methods and help in the healing process.

This was a land of contrasts and angry people: the teenagers, who never had a childhood, hating the restrictions that a country in re-building mode offered; the teenagers who were forced to live in the West away from their parents and forced once again to engage with what was to them a foreign country – and so backward! Disintegrating homes and family ties. My heart broke to see such grief and disconnectedness.

Ancient families. No more.

****

They will rebuild the ancient ruins
and restore the places long devastated;
they will renew the ruined cities that have been
devastated for generations.

Isaiah 61 v 4

Chapter Twenty Seven

Making Connections
Germany (1996)

The lights of Frankfurt spread out below. Soon I'll pass through the airport, catch the train, and head for Wiesbaden. Later I'll head to Stuttgart on my first speaking tour of southern Germany.

I know my subject (What is God doing in the Middle East?) but I don't know any Germans. How to connect with my audiences? I need a clue. What is this country going through at present?

I read in *Inflight* magazine about an exhibition now touring the country. It is lifting the lid on the possibility that ordinary soldiers are guilty of war atrocities—not only the Gestapo and the SS. In some quarters this is being hailed as an important admission. Other people struggle with their identity, even fifty years after the end of the Second World War. Is this something I could speak into?

There is only one person in my family who has connected with Germans, and that's my elderly father.

The day after I arrive I'm to address the students at DMZ, the German Missionary Institute. I stand before my first group of students and lecturers, about sixty in all. I have spoken to my interpreter and there are only a few people who do not feel comfortable in English. They will receive private translation on one side of the hall. I will speak without interruption. I cast my eyes upon my audience, mainly young people in their twenties. But there are older people here too, so I launch into my 'connection story'.

'When my father was twenty, he was stationed in North Africa during the Second World War. He was a gunner in the 2nd 7th Field Artillery of the Royal Australian Regiment. The year was 1940 and the enemy was the German Army, led by Field Marshall Rommel. (My audience just gaze at me. They did not expect this opening).

'One day my father became ill with dysentery. He walked into the desert, leaving his field gun emplacement and his crew. He carried his little spade. He dug a hole and perched over it, his khaki shorts bunched around his ankles and his bare bottom exposed to the sun. His stomach churned and pain filled him. He squatted there for some time, the sky above burning blue and white in the heat. Suddenly to his left came the familiar and dreaded wailing sound of a German fighter plane. My father clenched his eyes shut and held his breath.

"What a way to die," he thought. "How undignified!" He waited as the plane flew near. He waited as the plane started to circle around him. He had no alternative. There was nowhere to go. To his left, then behind, then coming up on his right, the screaming aircraft orbited around him, the guns silent. Again the plane circled and my father took a breath, opened his eyes, and looked up.

'The plane was circling low and he could see the German pilot looking down at him. Was he grinning? He was! And not only that, the German pilot gave my father the thumbs up. He dipped his wings in salute and flew back the way he had come.

'The undignified young Australian, squatting over a hole in the desert, completely vulnerable with his bare bottom towards the sun, was overwhelmed with gratitude to that pilot. And he's never stopped being grateful ever since.

'My father has told his family this story many times. Because of the mercy of that German pilot, my father returned to Australia, to his dear wife, had my three siblings and me, and is now a grandfather and a great grandfather. Dozens of people would not have been born if this German pilot had not been merciful to a young Australian in the North African desert in 1940.

'My father has always said how much he would have liked to have met that man and shaken his hand and thanked him.'

Night Journeys

I paused as I said this, my audience staring back at me. 'Today I speak to you as a grateful daughter on behalf of my father. I tell this story so that we can celebrate mercy and life together.'

I was then about to launch into my actual address when a woman about my age stood up and walked towards the podium.

She smiled as she came to me with her hand held out. 'My father fought with the German forces in North Africa,' she said. 'He was not your pilot, but I would like to shake your hand. On behalf of all the soldiers and airmen and all the people of Germany, to acknowledge one man's mercy to another.'

We shook hands and then hugged each other as the audience exploded into applause.

I had made my bridge. My father's experience cancelled my ignorance of not knowing any German people. That story and all subsequent speaking engagements during that tour of southern Germany paved the way for the open communication I needed so that I could connect with integrity with my audiences.

To the anonymous German pilot: 'Thank you'.

****

One generation will commend your works to another;
they will tell of your mighty acts.

Psalm 145 v 4

Chapter Twenty Eight

Making More Connections
Cornwall. U.K
(1996)

Barbara Murray is a long time friend I met in Coromandel Valley in 1979. For more than twenty years she lived in England. During a 17 day speaking tour I took three days off with her to explore Cornwall to find my lost relatives buried 'neath the sod. My cousin Annette Thornton had faxed me a genealogy of my family who had been born and died in Cornwall and Devon. I was to finish my journey in Cambridge the following week.

As we made our way to the West Country, we arrived at the Stoke Demerel Church in Plymouth, Devon, where George Burgess married Rebecca Samson in 1852. These lovers were from my Dad's mother's father's side. It was Sunday evening, so we nosed our way around the door and found a small group of people in a tight circle around a piano.

As they saw us walking towards them, I spoke up.

'Can we join you please?'

'That would be brilliant,' said Margaret Wright, a vibrant woman in an aqua blue jacket.

A slight woman with white curly hair said, 'I had just prayed that the Lord would send more men to our informal worship – and you two walked in!'

'The story of my life,' I said, and we were introduced all round and I moved towards an empty chair. Just as I got there the group called out in a loud voice, 'Don't sit there!'

Night Journeys

What a shock. Were they the sort of people who left a seat vacant in case Jesus should turn up?

Then I saw it. A gaping hole in the floor directly behind the wooden chair!

'One of our memorials fell off the wall last night. It would have killed the organist if it had happened during this morning's service.' That information came from Tony Barnard who was the warden who dealt with this sort of thing.

He continued, 'So we have put the chair there until we can get the carpenter in.'

We joined them in an intimate service of hymns and readings and then our new friends showed us over the church.

We were invited to touch the giant masts of great sailing ships that sailed out of Plymouth. In their retirement, these great masts now stood along the aisle, holding the church up!

Never seen that before.

I showed them my ancestor's marriage certificate.

4th of August, 1852
The Parish Church, Stoke Demerel,
in the County of Devon.
George Henry Burgess of full age, Bachelor, (Mariner)
Married Rebecca Samson of full age, Spinster.
Her father, Richard Samson (Blacksmith)
John Burgess (Farmer)

They shared our excitement and the linking of the past with the present. After that we stood in the Choir where George and Rebecca would have made their vows. We said a prayer of thanks and said our goodbyes.

****

After that friendly connection we headed further west to Redruth in the mining heart of Cornwall to visit the Parish Church of St. Uny, where my mother's side of the family had worshipped through the centuries.

St. Uny was a missionary priest from Ireland and his followers planted Celtic churches around Cornwall.

'He came over in a little boat and carried a brick,' Frank Chappel, told us in a broad Cornish accent. He had introduced himself when we entered the church grounds.

'All the Irish missionaries carried a brick that became their altar to the Lord,' he continued. 'The first church was a simple wooden building within an oval or circle of earthwork known as a '*Lan*'. '

Frank Chappel showed us the clear evidence of the 'lan' as we looked out from the present Norman tower to the northwest.

'For fourteen centuries people have been worshipping God here,' he told us.

I could imagine them singing praise, being built up in their faith, going courting, and giving and receiving in marriage, bearing infants, and being buried in the extensive graveyard.

Unlike the previous search in Devon, the marriage certificate I now had, was from my mother's side of the family. It read:

Samuel Hollow, Bachelor. Stone Mason of Clinton's Tce, Redruth,
and
Esther Merrett, Spinster of Hocking Court, Redruth,
were married
on
22nd July 1854

Frank took a look at the marriage certificate and pointed to the bridegroom's address. Samuel Hollow had lived in Clinton's Terrace in 1854.

Night Journeys

'That's my street!' said Frank. 'My family have lived in Clinton's Terraces for centuries. Your family and mine would have known each other very well!'

How about that? Another connection!

Before Frank left us he showed us the newly discovered grave of his great grandparents.

'I'm a member of the graveyard committee and we were clearing a huge swathe of ivy from a corner of the cemetery and there was the grave!'

In the photo I took of Frank beside his great grandparents' grave he looks so pleased with his find. So people are still discovering their ancestors' graves even in their own churchyards!

There we sat, Barb and I on the lid of a raised tomb, eating the most delicious Cornish pasty we had ever tasted. It was big and fat with lots of potato and pumpkin and other vegetables inside its soft, not flaky, pastry shell. Through the rising steam I sited a gravestone with the name *Jane May* deeply cut into it.

I took a sudden breath. Jane May! A woman by that name was listed on the genealogy on my father's side. But we were here in Redruth church looking at where my mother's relatives were married – not my father's!

And we discovered Jane - from the other side of the ancestral tree. I took out the genealogy and there were the names of Jane May and her husband John May.

The tombstone, as tall as me on my knees, stood humbly in the grass. It wasn't long before I was on my knees and Barb beside me. She found some slate and dug down with it to find if husband John was there. (She didn't expect to dig him up, just his inscription.) As she wiped her hands over the inscription, it offered up his dates.

John May
1766 - 1852

Raylene Pearce

The dates coincided with the information I'd been sent. We discovered that John was five years younger than Jane and lived a further nineteen years. Shortly after he died, their son John May immigrated to Australia in 1854 as a stone mason and worked on the cottages built into the hillside in Burra Burra, South Australia. These were the people on my father's side. So all those years ago, my mother and father's families were married, and buried in the same church. They would have known each other! Samuel Hollow and Esther (my mother's relatives) were married at St Uny's in 1854. John May (Dad's relative) was buried in the churchyard of St Uny's in 1852. I wonder if the families attended each others' ceremonies?

Now we were making connections.

It wasn't until 1940 that my mother Marjorie Hollow married my father, Ray Greenslade. Long before the young couple met in Adelaide South Australia their families would have known each other in Redruth, Cornwall.

But the greatest thrill of all was still to come.

I knew that ancestors on my mother's side were Christians, but have had no proof from Dad's side.

Now I had it!

Here is Jane May's epitaph.

Sacred to the Memory of
Jane May
Born in 1761,
Died in 1833
She died triumphing
in Christ her righteousness,
and now is the happy possessor
of an inheritance
incorruptible,
undefilable,
which fadeth not away.

135

Night Journeys

Have you ever seen a tombstone with the word 'happy' on it?

Can you imagine how I felt to have discovered this woman who shared the same experience of faith as me. Who shared the same narrative of faith action and expectation as mine! The eternal truth of the gospel carved in stone. No one has the words 'triumphing in Christ' on their tombstone unless that reflects their life. Her family must have recognised such attributes.

To know that her prayers, prayed on earth and in heavenly places have not been in vain. To realise that a woman called Jane May has been an intimate but unknown part of my spiritual heritage. I then thought of the future and how these dear folk were about to become great, great, great, great, great grandparents to my son's child!

(Holly was born the year of the discovery of her ancestor, and was named Holly May, after Jane May.)

More connections!

We speak of the Community of Saints in our Creeds. In the ancient churches of the Middle East and Mediterranean, the people acknowledge the saints that have gone before in personal terms. They acknowledge them as part of the worshipping community and include them in their church services and in their greetings.

I knew that my Mother and Nanna Bowey had gone into the very presence of Jesus and now were *'the happy possessors of an inheritance incorruptible, indefilable and which fadeth not away.'* Now I had others to look forward to when it was my turn to leave time and space and enter the other side of eternity – outside of time and space - into the very presence of God.

Now I see that my family's spiritual heritage in the saints goes much further back than I knew, on both sides of the family.

****

A week later I was preaching at the morning service at St Andrews Church in Cambridge and the minister asked me to preach again that night. I had already had a lunch meeting with students and an afternoon meeting with more students. So I had a brief rest and then asked God to give me a message.

I had been warned that many of the same people who heard me that morning would be in this huge church for the night service. Nothing in particular came to mind, but I had lots of stories about what Jesus is currently doing in the Middle East, and I had a strange peace about it all.

The Minister explained to the congregation that their studies on Zephaniah could wait as he had asked me to speak again. They would use the same New Testament reading as planned. Then an elder went to the elaborate lectern and read out my great-great-great-grandmother's epitaph!

****

1 Peter, Chapter 1 v 3 & 4

Blessed be the God and Father of our Lord Jesus Christ,
which according to his abundant mercy
hath begotten us again into a lively hope,
by the resurrection of Jesus Christ
from the dead,
*To an inheritance incorruptible and undefiled,
and that fadeth not away,
reserved in heaven for you.*

King James Version, published in 1611
Oxford University Press

****

Night Journeys

It was one week since we found the tombstone, but my connection with this congregation was established. I told them of my discovery the week before and used that scripture as the basis of everything I shared. My colleague, Diana, who was driving for me this time, said she had never heard me speak so well.

As we drove out the next morning, my throat closed up. I lost my voice. It was the end of three weeks' continuous speaking. Now was the time to return to the Middle East, write my reports, set up follow-up meetings and interviews, and rest my vocal cords.

(Wouldn't Mr Bennett be surprised? He remembered me for talking all the time. But Jesus redeemed this talkative girl and transformed her into a disciplined, confident speaker.)

****

Chapter Twenty Nine

Two days in the life of an Aussie Traveller
London (1990's)

Thurs May 11th
9.15am   BUS to South Bromley Station
9.30am   TRAIN to Victoria Station, then
                TUBE (Circle Line East) to Westminster
                TUBE to Embankment, change to
                TUBE (Northern line) south to Waterloo
                WALK to Partnership House
                BUS to Mildmay Hospital
                TAXI to Liverpool St Station
6pm   TRAIN to South Bromley
7pm   CAR to Sussex
12midnight   CAR to Bromley

Friday, May 12th 1995
9.10am   BUS to South Bromley Station
9.30am   TRAIN to Victoria, then change
                TUBE to Stockwell, then change
                TUBE northern line to Kennington
                WALK to The Company
                WALK to Vauxhall Station
                TRAIN to Teddington
                CAR to Gobram
                CAR to Victoria Station
10.20pm   TRAIN to South Bromley
11.15   CAR to Bromley

Night Journeys

Cameo on the Tube

He was about ten years old, fat, and black. He sat opposite me and as the tube started up he dug his hands into the huge pockets of his out-sized parka. First came packets of potato chips and lots of lollies, followed by a handful of leaflets to win holidays in the Canary Islands. Then came the cans of drink. One after another he transferred his loot into a giant carry bag between his feet. At one point, as he began work on his other pockets, I caught his eye and lifted my eyebrows. He never flicked an eyelid, or changed the deadpan expression on his face. Neither did he slow down in his transferring project. As the tube drew into the next station he hitched the bag over his shoulder, jacket somewhat lighter now, and made his way out. The only thing missing was the roll of a receipt!

****

Going the Wrong Way in the Good ol' U.K.
FIRST DAY: Heathrow to Wales

The plane banked through the thick clouds, landing without a shudder on the wet tarmac. Airport procedures passed without a hitch. Soon I was dragging my huge case onto a bus to Kenning's Car Hire and picking up a little black Fiesta.

Onto the street, cross the first intersection, turn at the mini round-a-bout (the first of dozens that were to dog my journey) then back to the same intersection, turn left, past the blue building, then the brown, get onto the overpass and onto the road to the M4. Missed the overpass, realised that I wasn't in sight of the M4, whipped into a MacDonald's and spoke to the first of many, many people from whom I asked directions. The man knew not where the M4 was, as he explained he was new to these parts, but a lady with a European accent seemed to know and pointed me to a stream of traffic in the far distance across a huge paddock.

Finding myself racing along the M4, I started to settle down and enjoy myself, wondering why there were no speed signs. Spent the next few hours merrily passing everyone in the middle lane who seemed to be dawdling at a boring 70 miles per hour, then into the outside lane, passing a few more, then nipping into the middle lane again.

All went well, until leaving a comfort stop. I was unsure in what direction Wales was on the M4. I took a guess. Happily driving along, I started to notice that the Junction Point numbers were decreasing instead of increasing. I realised for the first of what was to be a time of cosmic confusion along this same stretch of the M4 between Junction 30 and 32 that I found myself going the wrong way. How can anyone find the right direction without the sun?

Once in Wales, total confusion reigned. After stopping for petrol I found myself going back to Cardiff instead of on to Swansea. The signs on either side of that stretch of road had become very familiar with a Welsh word of about thirty characters. It was some time before I realised that it was the same word meaning REST STOP – in whatever direction you were going! No help at all.

Arriving on the outskirts of Swansea I was expecting to have trouble finding my way. But through the teaming rain, the heavy fog and squinting through my new multi-focals to peer at the map on my lap, and without having to ask any Welsh people how to get there, I made it!

SECOND DAY – Wales to Wales

Not so the following day.

Having lingered over breakfast with Jo and Jack White, whose son worked with us in Egypt, I was running late before I ever left their house. Once again the rain and fog, plus inadequate wipers, added to the watery view.

First thing was to turn the wrong way.

Second thing was to correct it and to discover there was no right hand turn.

Third thing was to try the next street and end up driving through Swansea proper instead of the ring route.

Asked the grand total of five people, 'Where is Bridgend?'

They all began their discourse with, 'You are going the wrong way'.

Soon I was hopelessly lost. A man walking over a crossing with his head firmly encased in his umbrella was the next person to tell me I was 'going the wrong way' and kindly pointed back the way I had come!

'Lord help me!'

Eventually, half an hour after I was supposed to be already at Bridgend, I entered the dreaded M4, leaving as directed at the Pyle Junction, to turn right at the first round-a-bout. Other intersections materialised like mushrooms after rain. I was on the wrong side of the M4, in – wait for it – completely the wrong direction. I had gone right at what wasn't the first round-a-bout, but what looked like one.

Finally, one hour after I should have arrived, I drove through the gates of the Evangelical Bible College of Wales, to be resuscitated with coffee. I proceeded to have a really good meeting over lunch as I had completely missed the class I was to address.

****

Raylene Pearce

…the Spirit helps us in our weakness.
We do not know what we ought to pray for,
but the Spirit himself intercedes for us
with groans that words cannot express.
And he who searches our hearts knows the mind of the Spirit,
because the Spirit intercedes for the saints
according with God's will.

Romans 8 v 26 – 27

Chapter Thirty

Planes, Trains and ... still going the Wrong Way!

Altogether during that October I went by car from Heathrow to Swansea, then to Bristol and Bath. I went north to Yorkshire, Blackpool, and to Nottingham, to meet prospective workers, to speak in churches, and stay at colleges like the Northumbria Bible College.

I had to catch 17 trains during this trip.

****

Edinburgh Anyone?

Now I'm on Berwick-on-Tweed station after staying and speaking at the Bible College in Northumbria.

I'm going to Edinburgh – or so I thought.

'The next train entering the station is going to Edinburgh.' At least that's what I thought the scrambled voice on the Tannoy said. So I followed everyone else who was waiting on the platform, (they all changed sides so I just followed them). Not wanting to be the only person left on the station I got on the train.

After dragging my 20kg case along the aisle I checked with a couple, 'Are you going to Edinburgh?'

They looked at each other and looked at me, looked at their tickets, looked at each other and then me again and said in a strong American accent, 'We're going to London.'

Yipes! Before I could get off, the train started off to London, first stop Newcastle! A dear lady conductor allowed me to use the phone

Raylene Pearce

on board and I was able to connect with *The Company* people who were to meet me in Scotland.
While sitting at Newcastle station I overheard two ladies chatting. One said, 'I shouldn't be allowed out by myself. I was supposed to be on the previous train but I was waiting on the wrong platform!' That made me feel better. I was as mad as the rest of the Geordies. I got to Edinburgh only two hours late.

****

To the ends of the Earth

During the next days I stayed the night at St Andrews University, encouraging students on future possibilities of work in the Middle East, and then to the Glasgow Bible College. I was driven to Glenshee in Perthshire to speak at an (IVSF) Intervarsity Student Fellowship Camp where I stayed and connected with students from all over Scotland.
I remembered that in Acts 1 V 8 Jesus, after his resurrection said,

'But you will receive power when the Holy Spirit comes on you;
and you will be my witnesses in Jerusalem,
and in all Judea and Samaria,
and to the ends of the earth.'

And *to the ends of the earth* they sent me - to Stornaway in the Outer Hebrides! My best memory of that experience was sitting over her peat fire with Kirsty McDonald aged 96, praying the heavens down. (The women of the Brethren Church on the Islands of Lewis and Harris are forbidden by their church to pray in public, or out loud in the presence of men.) So whenever *The Company's* Scottish director in Glasgow came to visit, they made him an honorary woman! And being a good *Company* man, he was proud to be thus called!

Night Journeys

After I returned from *the ends of the earth* I took five trains from Glasgow to Bury-St-Edmunds to visit the parents of colleagues in Egypt, then by car driven by Diana to Cambridge, where I preached twice at the huge church of St Andrews. After London, and speaking at a Missions Day at Holy Trinity, Brompton, I flew home to Cyprus.

****

I spoke in front of 2,500 plus people, at 27 meetings in 29 days. Added 80 people to our mailing list and interviewed people for jobs and saw many interested people to follow-up and encourage. There was plenty of work to keep me going until I took the next night journey.

At one meeting after holding my audience in the grip of intense concentration a lady came up to me and said, 'My son thought you were marvellous. He said watching you was like watching *Neighbours*.'

Some things are sent to keep us 'umble.

****

> May God be gracious to us
> and bless us
> and make his face to shine upon us,
> that Your ways may be known on earth,
> Your salvation among all nations.
>
> Psalm 67 v 1 & 2

Chapter Thirty One

Lindisfarne Island
(2002)
Holy Island Blessing

Dear friends and supporters, Tineke and Paul Dodson, visited me in Cairo and gave me a wonderful gift. They paid for me to travel to England and go on Retreat on the Holy Island of Lindisfarne. It was a grace-gifted journey of spiritual refreshment. I made a Reflection Book with poems and photos, my Celtic blood rising with Trinity songs.

The Holy Island of Lindisfarne is a tidal island in the North Sea just below the Scottish border. The rhythm of the place is dictated by whether the island is cut off from the mainland by treacherous waters, or joined by the receding tides leaving the causeway free for traffic. This place has strong links with St Aiden who founded the first mission station on Holy Island.

One of the reasons I wanted to stay in this holy place was the journey of faith I have made since living in the ancient land of Egypt. I experienced the direct connections between the Coptic and Celtic peoples.

At Durham Cathedral, I saw a high standing stone Celtic cross with base relief carvings from top to bottom on each of the four sides. On one side was St Matthew, then John the Baptist, then Jesus Christ with animals at his feet. The Latin writing around this carving said, 'The beasts in the desert adore Christ'. On another side were St Paul and St Anthony in the desert of Egypt. (The Desert Fathers, Paul and Anthony, were two of the first monks.) Then Mary and baby Jesus on the donkey with Joseph leading in the flight to Egypt.

Egyptian missionaries came to Ireland in the first centuries of the expansion of Christianity, so I see a complete circle from my Celtic roots and the Coptic peoples with whom I now live and serve. It's a lovely connection reflected in the art-work and Christian expression of both peoples.

I was spiritually guided by the co-host of 'The Open Gate' guesthouse of the Community of Aiden and Hilda. I met David Adam the rector of St Mary's and I have his book 'Flame in my heart – St Aiden for today'. I also met Ray Simpson who signed his book 'Exploring Celtic Spirituality'. I had brought Ray an icon made by the present monks of the monastery of St Paul on the Red Sea. He was thrilled. I encouraged him to visit the Desert Monasteries.

The Monastery of St Paul beside the Red Sea

The highlight of the precious time was the two days I took off early with my Bible, notebook, some fruit, and six hours of just 'being' with God and his beautiful creation. I don't think I have ever felt so close to nature, the birds calling and swooping along the cliffs, the seals singing, rabbits bouncing, lambs munching, tides turning and me lying on my back in sand dunes or in tufted patches of long grass watching the dance of the clouds.

Or sitting on rocks locking eyes with a particularly friendly seal, or on my tummy in an ancient quarry picking through fossil shale and gathering crinoids, fossils of plants growing on the ocean floor that can be strung into beads. Cuthbert's beads. Also, for the first time in my adult life, I did not feel overwhelmingly lonely on a beach. This was a gift from God as He lovingly revealed Himself in fresh ways to His daughter in this Holy Place.

Here are some of my Celtic songs and poems:

HOLY ISLAND CRADLING

I'm lying on Holy Island
I'm cradled on Holy Ground
cushioned on white sand dunes
in the Father's arms I'm found.
I'm lying on Holy Island
long grasses gently sway
with sounds of birds and sea and wind
Jesus comes to me this day.

I'm lying on Holy Island
the Spirit comforts me
He lets me know that it's OK
for me to be just me.
I'm lying on Holy Island
completely calm and free
restored and ever grateful
to the Island, and 'The Three'.

Night Journeys

SEA TALKING

It wasn't the sound of sea on sand
or sound of sea on pebbles.
But sounds of deep disturbances
of churning, heaving levels.
Of channels deep and treacherous
the sea made me aware
of life's challenges and changes
of moments rich with care.
The sea talked.
Voices from many directions
crying out.
The sea talked
and I didn't like it.
Crying in.

Later,
after Compline
back to the beach I go.
The tide has receded
peace has returned
channels no longer dangerous
sandbanks are exposed
and on them
the seals sit.
And sing.

Raylene Pearce

BEING GRATEFUL
Thank you Lord for this time of silence
of nature and You
and the North Sea calm and grey.
The sounds of waves on sand.
Even drops of rain
washing my face.
Maybe I will have the fun
of raising my umbrella.

CUTHBERT'S BEADS
I'm hunting Cuthbert's beads,
hunting Cuthbert's beads,
lying on my stomach
in search of Cuthbert's beads.

I'm singing Jesus songs
while finding Cuthbert's beads.
I've a little pile of Cuthbert's beads
while singing Jesus songs.

Now in the silence looking
at 'crinoid' fossils raised
God did this long ago for Cuthbert
so he could pray and praise!

Night Journeys

COMMUNING WITH BROTHER SEAL
I'm sitting on a cliff-face
watching seals at play
their black noses point this way.
I could sit and watch all day.

Sun catches heads reflecting
shining skin, white cheeks gleaming,
spotted tummies now appearing.
I'm sitting here just watching.

Brother seal his eyes attaching
to mine is quite enchanting
I think it's my black beret attracting.
He probably thinks I'm a relative!

RYTHMS
The tide turns, the buses return.
And we who are staying
give a sigh
and embrace the quietness.
God's gift to our rhythm of life
on Lindisfarne.

STORY TELLERS
Ancient stones
tell wonderful stories.
Lindisfarne Priory
a place to explore
and remember
with thanksgiving.

Raylene Pearce

LANDING ZONE
The North Shore
peaceful and clean.
A healing place.

400 miles out to sea…
Norway.
Seventh century Vikings came
taking the gospel back
with the 50 slaves they stole.

I think upon those days….
"Lord have mercy
Christ have mercy".
People torn apart
yet made whole in You.

Here in tranquility
I lay upon the dunes
watching grey clouds dancing
and white birds winging
Bathed in silent sounds of love.
I think upon those days…
"Lord have mercy
Christ have mercy."
People torn apart
yet made whole in You.

The North shore.
A healed place.

Night Journeys

LINDISFARNE JOURNEY
Thank you Lord for life now.
Thank you Lord for life then.
The then and the now.
Interchanging.
Everlasting.
Enriching me on my forever walk
with you.

THANK YOU LORD
for special friends who gave
so that I might be blessed
by this Holy Place.

July 5^(th) to 12^(th) 2002
This Holy Island of Lindisfarne.
Outpost for the gospel to my
ancestors in the 6^(th) century.

Thank you Lord for sending
Aidan, Cuthbert, Hilde and others
so that we might have the
light of the glorious gospel -
Jesus.

****

Raylene Pearce

Another Island - Mediterranean Sea

Imagine arriving in a country you have never been to before. Everything goes well. There's a man at the airport with your name written clearly with the name of the Hotel on a large card.

The driver takes you to the Hotel. It's 3a.m. Everything is closed up. The night watchman you can see through the glass door can't find his keys – he's not pleased to be interrupted from his sleep under the counter. Eventually they are found and there is an altercation between the taxi driver called Michael and the night watchman. In Maltese.

Michael turns to you and tells you that you are not expected. There are no rooms. Your name is not on the list although the Hotel had arranged the taxi to collect you!! What to do? They start thumbing through a dog-eared phone directory and ring several numbers. Finally there is a Hotel nearby with an empty room. It's now 4 a.m.

That's the way I began my one-day visit on the Island of Malta enroute back to Egypt. I spent the afternoon with Alison who is the daughter of Barbara Murray, and her family. We went to their church in a pleasant hotel ballroom and after spending the rest of the day with my friends, my driver Michael drove me back to the airport.

He wanted me to see his village. So we drove to his church lit up with a million lights to celebrate the Festival of St Paul who was shipwrecked there a couple of thousand years ago …….. sort of felt like I identified with him a bit.

> Once safely on shore,
> we found out that the island was called Malta.
> The islanders showed us unusual kindness.
> They built a fire and welcomed us all
> because it was raining and cold.
>
> Act 28 v 1 & 2

Chapter Thirty Two

Connecting Again
England (1996)

He was in his seventies, with a cheery face and cheery eyes. He was determined to show me the Illuminations. I, being the gracious guest, acquiesced as he, grabbing my hand, trotted off. This was high adventure in a quaint old place called Blackpool.

I remember as a child hearing a recitation from an English chap with a Yorkshire kind of accent, recite a comic poem about the pier at Blackpool, pronounced with long, drawn-out vowels. Now here I was, being dragged along by sprightly Stan, walking stick in one hand and me in the other. It was no leisurely stroll along the promenade but a brisk walk with Stan pointing out with his stick the various lights arched over us. The Illuminations were shaped as bells, holly, and other Christmassy images. I was under-awed, but true to type made the expected positive response to such illuminated glory. There was also a tower to be pointed out for me to exclaim over.

Satisfied that I had seen and approved this important seaside sight, Stan reluctantly lead me back one street from the modest and not-illuminated Baptist Church. On arrival, we found my colleague Diana in the dark, banging on the back door trying to be heard by the people inside. With due apologies, Stan gave the door a mighty wallop with his broad shoulder and the three of us bounded into the bleak, hollow-sounding hall. There are many such halls throughout the world and this is just one of them.

Raylene Pearce

I was the overseas guest speaker to a group of enthusiastic and welcoming elderly folk, gathered for a shared finger-food dinner followed by me for dessert. Copious cups of tea and tiny cucumber-and-cheese sandwiches were consumed with gratitude.

Prior to meeting Stan, Diana and I had driven from London to Blackpool to discover the place had been taken over by the police force. There were roadblocks everywhere, which made our endeavours to get to the bed-and-breakfast allocated us, a journey of discovery. We found out from an obliging policeman that it was the 1998 Conservative Party's annual conference. Being political morons we had no idea of the eminent personages who were flooding into the place. This would later explain why there were such low numbers who showed up at my conference. A small group of faithful Christians gathered in competition with the great Conservative Party up the street.

Diana, the Office Secretary for our Media Ministry in the UK, and I had been given the address of members of the congregation who had the gift of hospitality and owned a B&B. We parked in a narrow street and walked up the minuscule path to a doll's house, decked out in concrete and shells made into amazing naturalistic shapes. These shapes were on every surface of ground, the fence and the outside wall of the residence. The tiny garden was also concreted with mosaics of shell and broken dishes.

Looking along the street that led towards the thin strip of blue of the Irish Sea was row after row of what looked like doll's houses. Not to be outdone by the Illuminations along the seafront, all the dwellings of this famous holiday resort enveloped their homes with bric-a-brac and B&B signs, welcoming all travellers. We noted that each front window was a bay, beautifully draped in pretty curtains, encircled by blinking fairy lights and in the centre a frilly lamp, lit up to invite us within.

Do I sound condescending? I guess I do, because I had never experienced such a twee environment and somehow felt claustrophobic even before I went inside. The tiny entrance was imposed upon by a narrow staircase and was crowded with a large group of jolly holidaymakers jerkily moving upwards, their cases bumping against the balustrade. We were on the first floor and very grateful we were—until we saw our room. It was the size of a double bed. And a double bed filled the room. There was a thin dressing table on which we piled our overnight bags. We made our escape as soon as we could, trying not to look at each other. Needless to say, neither of us slept that night. Diana kept getting the giggles and I kept getting the burps.

****

Earlier that evening a young couple had driven over from Liverpool for an interview with me for a position with our magazine in Egypt.

After giving my enthusiastic talk, I left the elderly group and met the young people in the minister's study. I had their job descriptions on my laptop as well as their application papers and references. This couple had been attracted by the dual package of journalism and information technology that the Magazine and Media department offered.

We were about an hour into the interview when the young woman said, 'I see you are with *The Company*. Were you ever in Northern India?'

'I was in Missouri.'

'Did you stay with the Mackintoshes?'

'Yes.'

'When were you there?'

'February 1991.'

She then said haltingly, shyly, 'While you were there, was there anyone else staying there at the same time?'

I stopped, stared at her and slowly remembered…'Yes, there was a young woman…'

'IT WAS ME!!' she squealed.

Felicity jumped out of her chair, I jumped out of mine, and we hugged each other, the young husband sitting there with a startled look on his face. Laughing and crying, Felicity and I clung to each other as we bounced up and down.

When we calmed down, she continued, 'After you put me on the train at Dehra Dun I went directly to Varanasi to the convent of the *Sisters of our Lady of Providence* – a sister convent to the Catholic school I attended in England. I was saved there. The Sisters lead me to Jesus. Through the Holy Spirit directing me, I left for Kathmandu staying with some contacts you'd given me en route in Butwal. I then went to Calcutta where I worked for Mother Teresa for a month. Then it was time to return to England. I studied journalism at Liverpool University and it was there I met Mark.

(Many years later when Felicity was checking the text of this chapter, she said, 'I count you as a valuable link in the chain of events that led me to Christ - you should put that in!')

And now, seven years after that meeting in Northern India there we were in Blackpool! It was almost too much to get our minds around. We strolled arm in arm down to the local pub to share the stories of our lives and how we had come together in the most unlikely of places.

Mark later said that when he watched us jumping around the study hugging each other he thought, 'We're in, we're in'.

The following year I was on a speaking tour of the UK and I visited Mark and Felicity in Liverpool to preach at their church and to check on their application progress. This time Felicity was pregnant. At the same time my first grandchild was born in Adelaide, South Australia and given the lovely name of Holly May. It was eighteen months before Mark and Felicity came to Egypt and by then Mark was carrying in his backpack a little girl called Holly Joy!

****

Night Journeys

Here I was, a year later joining them. At the time I recollect being so grateful. My flat was across the passage from theirs and some mornings little Holly Joy would trot across the corridor for a morning cuddle. Not only had we come full circle in meeting up again, in my personal grief at not being near my own grandchild, Holly May, another little Holly had been provided. What a God-given connection!

Why was the landlord prepared to bring down the rent from one thousand pounds to seven-fifty a month? We all saw it as God's provision. And it was.

****

'I will fear no evil, for you are with me;'

Psalm 23 v 4b

Part Six

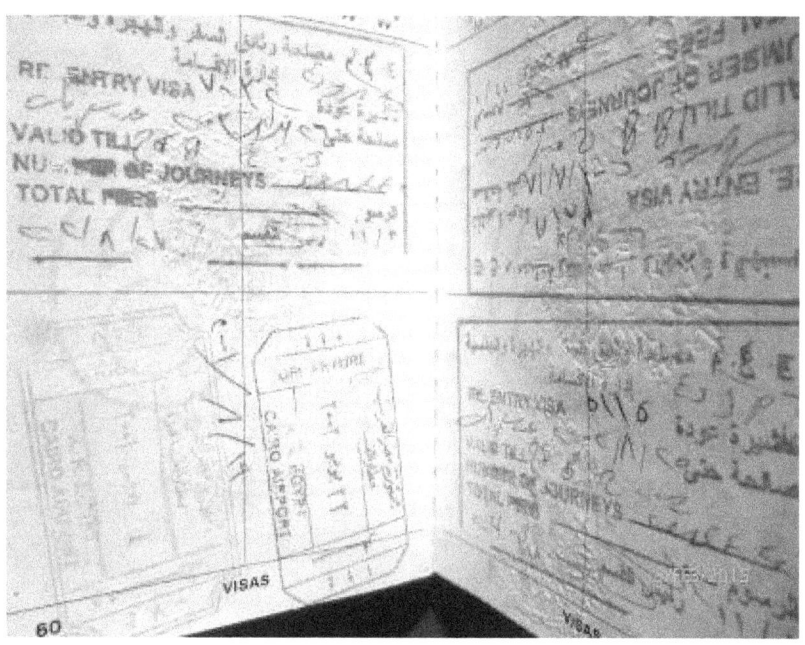

Egypt

Chapter Thirty Three

One Thousand and One Egyptian Nights
Burps in the Night (1990's)

I drag my old flaccid case out of the lift and into my office.

Robert Williams is waiting. 'You don't have to do this, Raylene. There's a major risk.'

Today I am leaving on my eleventh trip to Egypt from Cyprus. Each time I travel in my job I double as a courier. Cyprus is like a hub in the wheel of the Middle Eastern world, a jewel of an island in the Mediterranean Sea. From the Greek side of Cyprus we leave Larnaca airport, flying in all directions. I sometimes think of my home as being at the end of the runway although I live in Nicosia in the centre of the island, and the airport is an hour away near the coast.

Whenever I travel, colleagues from sister organisations leave piles of mail to be taken. Then it's picked up at the end of the journey by arrangement. The mail can be birthday gifts for children, books, magazines, and Christian literature, things that are often lost in transit through regular postal channels. Sometimes there is no risk, except muscle strain from carting heavy loads, but other times the risk is higher.

This is one of them. A Bible Society wants me to take the entire batch of the master videotapes for the entire Bible. Master tapes are larger and thicker videos than usual ones and there are about seventeen of them. From the master, the Bible Society will copy the entire Bible in video form for distribution among the churches. When you work in countries where there is no freedom of religion, any transaction of this nature is always a challenge.

Night Journeys

My case is only half-filled to allow for the tapes to nestle within my clothes for the ten-day stay. I am also taking for friends an assortment of groceries and medications still not available in Cairo.

'You have a choice,' says Robert. 'You can declare the tapes and hope that they will not be confiscated. If they are, it will be the last we see of them.'

And the last you would see of me, I think.

But instead I say, 'I don't want that to happen. I know how long the project has taken.'

Illiteracy is still a major problem for much of the Middle East. To have the entire Bible acted out with the scriptures subtitled in Arabic is a wonderful way of allowing Christians, who make up about ten percent of Egyptian people, access to the Scriptures in a creative way.

'Here's the list of every tape,' Robert goes on. 'Keep it with you and if your case is opened you can show the list and hopefully this will help plead your cause.'

Interrogation, you mean, I think to myself.

Then Robert looks at me gravely. 'You know that there is a real risk. If things go wrong you won't be allowed in. You'll be blacklisted. It will end your work here as you know it.'

Now he's talking my language. I didn't read all those spy novels for nothing. But in reality, every trip turns my insides into a butter churn. I used to get an upset stomach catching a bus to the city from my home in Brighton, a half-hour journey from Adelaide in South Australia. I hated catching public transport and here I was doing it for a living! This trip would be a major tummy-tumbler.

When I was twelve I discovered heroes: Mary Slessor of Calabar in Africa and Gladys Aylward of China. Elizabeth Fry of the prison work in London and Florence Nightingale. Then WW2 heroines like Nancy Wake, Violet Szasbo, and Odette Churchill, all double agents working behind enemy lines. When I was older I read every LeCarre novel. The books about Dr Helen Roseveare's work in Africa stirred my resolve to live a life on the edge of my comfort zone. I have admired the strength and courage of women ever since. God's women are not wimps.

I accept this assignment. I kneel on my office floor and commence packing the contraband. At risk is my job. I have to have freedom of access into Egypt. I am the Personnel Director to international people, supporting Christian Egyptians. No access. No job. I am only living on Cyprus because that's where the international office is. I travel almost every month, back and forth to Turkey, Jordan, Lebanon, Egypt, and Europe. I want to keep my job. I love my job!

On these journeys there is always at the back of our minds the knowing that for the items we carry, all that would happen to us expatriates would be expulsion. But it's our national colleagues we seek to protect. Once taken into custody one never knows if they will be seen again. Beatings are the prerequisite of entry into the gaols. Read 'torture' for 'interrogation'.

At four pm the service taxi comes. I pile in with my no longer flaccid case, stiff with the precious cargo wrapped up in my undies and other goodies. The journey takes an hour. As we pick up people waiting by shops in villages, postage and newspapers are exchanged. It's an interesting way to see what lies beyond the freeways of the island.

There is a sandstorm off the Sahara. All planes going in that direction are grounded. I settle into my latest *whodunit*. Seven hours pass in the smoke-laden atmosphere of Larnaca Airport. A fascinating place with 'no smoking' signs all over the walls. I ask a shop assistant why the signs are there when they are ignored.

'Oh the government make us put the signs up but no one likes them, so we ignore them,' he says.

Much later we finally board *Egypt Air*. It is now after midnight. All goes well until the flight attendant presents me with the only choice of snack: a stale bread roll with a limp cheese slice and something that says, 'This is not ham.'

I take a bite, swallow, and there it stays, somewhere halfway down my oesophagus. Weak coffee makes no difference. Thumping my chest only makes the lady beside me in her flowery *hijab* look at me in alarm. There the lump sits and the burps begin.

The plane lands. I shuffle down the aisle and step into the bus to the airport terminal.

'Burp.'

I wait in a long line for passport check.

'Burp.'

I present my worn passport full of stamps to the gentleman at the counter.

'Burp.'

I'm asked to wait the other side of the line while a lady with a dark-blue *hijab* enters my details into a computer. I watch through the curtain and see the green glow of rows and rows of entries. This is my eleventh trip in, and with ten out. My file is increasing.

'Burp.'

I finally get my passport back.

'Burp.'

Now to get a trolley. Since my last visit the price has gone up. I grope in my pocket, draw out a wad of dirty one-pound notes. I extract five. The familiar smell of well-worn money tickles my nose. It's starting to really feel like Cairo.

Leaning on my trolley, I enter the crowd as they gather around the carousel. I have learnt a strategy. Don't look at your case. Don't even appear to notice your case, even as it approaches you. Look totally disinterested. On previous trips I have taken note of my red case moving towards me. Before I have been able to grab it, a fellow in a white turban will swing it off the carousel and hold it in one hand. The other held out towards me, waiting for *baksheesh*. Not until a couple of notes sit on his hand will my case sit on my trolley.

Here comes the case. Don't look. Don't look. Grab it. Swing it over. Plonk it on the trolley. Start to move towards the customs queue.

'Burp.'

I have never been searched by customs. I have never had my case opened during my trips into Middle Eastern countries. In all my trips from Cyprus to Egypt, I have never been told to open my case, or have even had a search of my handbag. I approach each airport with a grin from ear to ear. I break all the rules. I smile. I look into the eyes of the customs officers.

I look so pleasant, and have perfected my reply to 'Why do you come here so often?' with '*Ana habeeb misr*'. 'I love Egypt.' Another smile. No worries.

But this time it's different. I'm really nervous.

'Burrrp.'

My turn. I hand over my passport. The young guy flips through the massive tome and asks me what I have in my bag.

'Oh just my stuff. Burp. Clothes, you know. Stuff I need.'

'Open the case.'

'Burp. You want me to open my case? Burrrrp.'

'Yes, would you please open your case.'

I bend down and gather the case in my arms. I plonk it onto the stainless steel ledge. I lean on it, exhausted from the effort. The customs officer watches me closely.

I force my face up to look into his. 'Burp.'

Still leaning on the case, I start to unzip. First the right-hand zip. Around it goes.

'Burp.' I look up again. 'Burrrp. Burrrp.'

Then the left-hand zip, my burps increasing. I'm still leaning on the case, looking up at him. This time as I look into his handsome face, I notice it's going through a change. He began with a healthy-looking light-brown countenance with signs of a faint beard around his chin. I now notice that he's looking a bit grey and sweaty and he's white around his mouth.

'Burrrrp.' This burp comes from way down in my gullet. It sounds ghastly; I have never burped like this before.

This time he recoils as I lean in closer.

Night Journeys

'Burrrp. Where … is … the … toilet? Burrrp!'
Before I know it he has grasped my case in both hands and with a great push sends it sailing down the stainless steel chute.
'That way,' he cries.
I grab the case, swing it onto the trolley, and leaning heavily on it, wheel myself out of his sight towards the rows of waiting taxis.

****

'Thank you God for your Guardian Angels.
'Thank you Lord, for my nervous stomach.
And thank you God, for burps.

****

'Taxeeee!'

****

I praise you because I am fearfully and wonderfully made;
your works are wonderful, I know that full well.

Psalm 139:14

Chapter Thirty Four

Still Mediterranean Hopping
Cross Keys

I made at least four pastoral visits a year to Cairo. As Personnel Director I visited all expats working in our organisation. I saw the children at school and after and had coffee with young mums and sat with the others at work. I was responsible for recruiting people to fill the specialist media positions and then to make sure they were cared for on location.

Whenever I visited Egypt I stayed with single women colleagues, usually in the suburb of Maadi. One such friend, Ananeke, was someone whom I had come to know and love over the years. A wonderful person who lived many years in Cairo, working with disabled children and their families. She set up the first ever preschool for disabled children in the city. She held open house and I came and went, as I needed to. All I had to do was let her know when I'd be coming and check to see if she had room for me.

Flights between Cyprus and Egypt were always night journeys, as they were a part of longer flights between Europe and Africa or Asia.

Ananeke was a very laid-back woman. Nothing fazed her. So when I got to her flat in the middle of the night I'd bang on her door until she woke. I did not have a key to her lock and Ananeke did not have a doorbell that worked.

After one longer than usual journey from the airport to Ananeke's flat I walked past the sleeping *bowab*. The doorkeeper slept under the

Night Journeys

stairs curled up in a brown blanket. I climbed the five flights of stairs, my case bumping behind me.

At Ananeke's flat, I banged on the door. Ananeke wasn't hearing me. It was now three thirty. In an hour's time the mosques would ring out the morning prayers. I did not want to spend the rest of the night on her doorstep. I had been travelling since four pm. All I wanted was a comfy bed.

Bang, bang.
Nothing.
I tried again.
Bang, bang, bang.
I stood back, looked at the door, 'Please God, help me.'
I took out my purse. I looked inside. I took out the only key I had.
My flat located in the district of Lykovitos, in the city of Nicosia, on the island of Cyprus.
I looked at it and shrugged.
I put it in the lock.
The key turned.
The door opened!
I tiptoed past Ananeke's room, her gentle snoring assuring me that she was at home. I made my way to the back bedroom and fell on the bed.

In the morning while Ananeke was making breakfast I popped my head around the kitchen door.

Not even blinking an eye, she said, 'Ready for coffee?'

Later that morning I tried my key again.
It would not fit!
God had come through for me again!

> The Lord is my shepherd I have everything I need.
> Psalm 23.1

Raylene Pearce

Chaotic Flight (2000's)

I'm returning to Egypt after Home Assignment. It's been an emotional time; a year since my father died. I'm always fragile when I leave my family anyway, especially straight after Christmas, but I chose to leave early because I wanted to attend a conference in my area of the world between Christmas and the New Year.

While lined up at Sydney airport, I was reminded of Egyptair flight 990 which crashed in the ocean after taking off from New York. Then, as now, this plane crash is still under investigation. Information available from the recovery of the black box reveals that a relief First Officer entered the cockpit when the Captain was absent and sent the plane into a nose-dive taking all 217 passengers with him.

Why was my mind triggered about this disaster?

As we lined up, the Egyptair crew entered the Checking In area, and in front of us all, one by one, had their photographs taken, then a group photo!

'Have you ever seen that before?' I asked the woman waiting in line behind me.

'No. Why are they doing that? Do you think it's about that Egyptair crash last year?'

'What I was thinking too – but it's very odd to do that in front of all the passengers. Surely there's somewhere an airline's crew can meet before they board the plane?'

'Makes you feel strange. Wasn't there a finding that a co-pilot committed suicide and caused the crash?'

'That's what I heard too. I took Egyptair because it was the cheapest.'

We gave each other a weak smile and proceeded, like lambs to the slaughter, to board the aircraft.

There's a lot of movement on Egyptair flights. The only people in our section who were buried in books or watching videos were Westerners and there were about a dozen of them. Otherwise the aircraft was full of Egyptians who aren't well known for their reading, but excellent in social intercourse.

I remember vividly our landing into Cairo. Someone in our section on the far side collapsed. The person sitting next to him started shouting at him, shaking him by the shoulders and thumping him. People got up and crowded around. Crew were nowhere to be seen. We were all supposed to be belted up ready to land. I pressed the button and heard several people doing the same. Someone pushed through the mob shouting loudly, and I hoped he was a doctor.

The plane started to descend, banking to the left and then the right, now losing height. The people swayed and some fell about as the plane began to land. Still no crew showed to get the people seated and to help the collapsed man. Eventually we landed with people falling all over the place. We Westerners sat belted up with eyes popping like gold fish.

The locals blocked the aisles and everyone seemed to have forgotten the poor collapsed man. The cabin crew finally appeared. The plane taxied for about five minutes, then stopped near the edge of the parking bays cut into the desert.

Buses will take us to the terminal. My strategy is to stay seated on the plane till the last people leave. Then I get on the bus, and stand close to the door. Arriving at the terminal, I usually find myself at the beginning of the passport control line.

I cannot comment as to the condition of the collapsed man as I got caught up in the airport procedures, but I do know that getting involved in strangers' traumas in Egypt can be dicey.

****

Raylene Pearce

One day I was crossing the road near my place – about six lanes of traffic. Actually, I'm not sure of the exact number of lanes as drivers weave in and out and fill up spaces in front of them. It's hard to work out where the lanes are. Drivers drive very freely and it's up to the drivers coming behind to give way and fit in with whatever is happening on the road ahead. Easy. No rules. Just watch out the front window. Excellent brakes. I never drove in Egypt. As a single person I never had the allowance to buy a car and there was only one Methuselah!

A group of us were about to step into the traffic (as you do) when the man beside me got hit by a mini bus and thrown over the front of a car. As I knelt down beside him I was shoved aside while the others pulled him to his feet!

I'd heard about this. If a person is knocked down by a car, bus, or donkey cart and can stay on their feet after the accident, then the person driving the car, bus, or donkey cart can continue on their journey. And I saw it happen. He stood up looking very dazed and wobbly. He was judged fit by the crowd, and the traffic continued as before.

****

> Though I walk in the midst of trouble
> you preserve my life;
> The Lord will fulfil his purpose for me;
> your love, O LORD, endures forever.

Psalm 138 v 7

Chapter Thirty Five

Hot Cairo Night

I was leaving the old Cairo Air Terminal building. Instead of going to the usual rank of taxi stands, I succumbed to the gentle influence of a pleasant young man who quoted me a low price to my destination in Maadi, south of Cairo. He took me to a waiting room nearby. There was a statue of Mary, the mother of Jesus, in the window and because it was a Christian group and the young chaps were cheerful and friendly I felt okay about it.

Soon a few other travellers arrived and we were ushered out into the car park. Instead of the expected taxi, a mini bus awaited us. Before I could change my mind, my case was lost among all the others. I could see that this was going to be a long night. No straight home route this time.

There were eight of us in the twelve-seater; cases and large boxes filled the boot, overflowed into the aisle, and piled on spare seats. The cheerful driver, Girgis, got us to introduce ourselves to each other. I remember there was a Swedish man on his first trip to Egypt, Sven Olson. There was a middle-aged American couple on their way to Upper Egypt on a cruise and a young Egyptian girl called Miral Ibrahim returning after many years in college in the US. She had more luggage than, I imagine, the Queen travels with.

We set off in the direction of the city. Sven Olson had forgotten the name of his hotel. He was sure he'd remember if he saw it in lights! So began our pub-crawl of downtown Cairo in the midnight hour.

'No, that's not it,' he'd say as he gazed out the window at a little hotel or a grand glitzy palace. This did not bother Girgis, who would gleefully drive off to the next option. After several stops, they both got out and went into a hotel to talk to the manager. To my relief and the relief of the other passengers too, Sven was given a room for the night. He'd go looking for the right hotel the next day.

We waved goodbye, and quickly disposed of the American couple at the Hilton overlooking the river. The Nile glittered with feluccas, age-old boats with sails, filled with partygoers. The city never sleeps, and a summer night entices people of all ages onto the river.

Norm Tucker took this great photo of Cairo at dusk

We left Tahrir Square in the centre of town, and joined the endless traffic flowing over the bridges. We crossed the island of Zamalek into Imbaba, on the far side of the Nile, completely in the opposite direction to where I had hoped to end up before the night was over. Imbaba is one of the highest populated areas of Cairo.

The bus came into a narrow sandy street and tried to turn a corner. It got stuck against a parked car. The neighbourhood was wide-awake. We were soon besieged by a crowd of witnesses, all giving advice, like the old guys at the cricket. Back and forth, back and forth went the bus, until it caved into the car. As the crunch reverberated throughout the minibus, the returning girl's family all turned up.

Night Journeys

With great excitement they swarmed like bees into the bus. They were unable to get to Miral's luggage, trapped in the concave back. Between weeping for joy, shouting and copious kissing, the family pulled out everything they could lay their hands on from the back. They dragged cases through the middle of the bus and out of the front door like a swarm of killer ants on the rampage. I managed to grab my case as I saw it travel along the aisle tucked under the arm of one of Miral's relatives.

But the bus was still stuck. It was now close to two a.m. and the neighbourhood was alive in celebration of Miral's return. Girgis gathered the men and they rocked the bus off the poor car and moved it into a position to continue the dropping off of passengers.

Eventually we were racing south along the Corniche. The Nile gleamed with reflected yellow streetlights on our right; the darkness of the City of the Dead was on our left. Soon everyone was dropped off. I moved up to sit alongside Girgis in the seat by the window, next to the door.

'You are beautiful.'

I ignored him. I kept looking out the window.

'You are beautiful.'

This time I looked and shrugged my shoulders.

'Are you married?'

'Yes,' I lied.

Silence, then once more.

'You are VERY beautiful.'

'*Aiwa*. Yes. *Anna jamila aiwi. Allatuul Corniche, menfudlak.* Yes, I am very beautiful. *Allatoon*. Straight ahead, thank you. Straight ahead along the Corniche.'

I then directed him to turn left at the midan, the roundabout by the BP service station. With a stern face I continued my directions in Arabic. Girgis was sulking now, but he obeyed my directions and I arrived at the gate to the garden of Ananeke's apartment.

I was cross with Girgis. He knew better than to chat up a lone woman on his bus.

Raylene Pearce

He drove off without any baksheesh — no tip this time.

****

> The LORD is my light and my salvation –
> whom shall I fear?
> The LORD is the stronghold of my life –
> of whom shall I be afraid?
>
> For in the day of trouble
> he will keep me safe in his dwelling;
> he will hide me in the shelter
> of his tabernacle
> and set me high upon a rock.
>
> Psalm 27 v 1 & 5

Norm Tucker's photo of the Corniche alongside the Nile

Chapter Thirty Six

Night desert ride

My grapefruit-size knee immobilises me against the plywood barrier between the seat and the bus door. Recently, I twisted my kneecap getting out of a car after a four-hour trip. Rip – and I knew radical damage had happened, a cartilage ripped, and fluid filling my knee and surrounding tissues.

I watch the darkening desert road ahead with growing horror as the manic bus driver passes everything in sight. The long road is choked with speeding vehicles, like the beginning of a Grand Prix, the drivers battling for pole position.

We are travelling from Mersa Matruah, on the Mediterranean coast near the Libyan border. We skirt the Qattara Depression where the Australian army, my father included, faced the Germans during the Second World War. Then, through the Great Western Desert to Cairo, in what is supposed to be a six-hour trip.

The overweight man next to me is pressing against me, squashing my aching head hard against the window. My fellow passengers, all Arab males, are intent on Jean-Claude Van Damme screaming out of the TV above my head. I turn my face to the sandblasted window, trying to avoid the monochrome images of the post-nuclear world. But they reflect back at me. There is no escape.

Four hours later I'm deposited in downtown Cairo with the injunction ringing in my ears of Fady's warning:

'Do not take a taxi. It's not safe for a woman alone. It's too late at night. Cross the road and catch a mini-bus.'

Raylene Pearce

By now my knee is as big as a rock melon. I hesitate before trying to cross the eight lanes of coloured lights streaming under the Sixth of October Bridge, to get to the mini-bus station.

Suddenly a man grabs my bag, throws it into the back seat of his taxi, and pushes me in. We merge into the traffic. It is 2.30 a.m. The city of Cairo is wide-awake, on this hot August night. The noise, at its usual high decibel, and the air full of lead and other pollutants, oddly reassures me. For the first ten minutes all is well. The driver is crouched over the steering wheel, filling the taxi with cigarette smoke, his radio wailing '*Habeebi, habeebi*' 'My love, my love'.

Imagine this is at night. This man was not the 'horror' driver of this story. This dear man was driving when Norm Tucker took this photo.

He meanders through the four lanes of traffic along the busy corniche, straddling the Nile. I lean back onto the warm plastic covered seat and watch the familiar scenes flash by, glad to be nearing home.

Night Journeys

Unexpectedly, the driver turns left into darkness. I grab hold of the back of the seat by the driver's head, my hand sticky on the plastic:
'*Men Fadluk, ana iza ......*' 'If you please. I want ....'
He doesn't let me finish and starts blasting away in a tirade of Arabic, both arms flaying the air. He puts his foot down, the swaying 'coffin on wheels' tearing through the blackened unfamiliar streets.
He's not using his lights!
Every now and then, approaching a corner, he flicks them on, almost taking a whitened sepulchre with us. No electricity in this part of the city – 'The City of the Dead'. Through the shape of domed tombs I glimpse the floodlit Citadel in my left window and feel a moment of relief. Something recognisable.
Another swerve, it disappears, and I'm left once more with no landmarks.

Would I ever be seen again?
No one knows where I am.
I'm totally at the mercy of the driver.
Is my taxi driver a good man?
He drives like a bat out of Dante's hell.
How many trips does he expect to make this night?
Maybe he's on a 'trip' of his own?

Only Fady's warning in my ears, 'Do NOT catch a taxi! There is no way of checking whom you are with and to where you are being taken. Catch the mini bus.'

I sway with each abrupt turning.
I feel the wings of angels.
I sink into their protection.
My twelve foot high, multi-coloured winged guardians.
I had forgotten they were there!
Thank you Lord.

The taxi circles the midan near my flat. I recognise my local *souk* (market) and the florist shop on the corner of my street.

Here it is – but during the day.

Relief pours in.
He's bringing me home!
He's not going to kidnap me!

I pay the extra ten pounds baksheesh.
I fumble with the key in my gate.
He backs into the empty street.

****

If you say, 'The Lord is my refuge,'
He will command His angels concerning you
to guard you in all your ways;
they will lift you up in their hands
so that you will not strike your foot against a stone.

Psalm 91 v 9

Night Journeys

Consequences

'That wasn't appropriate, Raylene. Fady should have known better than to have put you in that position. What was he thinking?' Nevine looked at me gravely.

The problems these expatriates brought upon themselves amazed Nevine, who had never once stepped out of her sheltered cultural boundaries.

Nevine, my best Egyptian friend, is thirty years of age. Before I complete my time in Egypt, she will break the taboo of never being separated from her family, even for one night. She will go away with me for a farewell weekend to a Desert Retreat Centre. Her husband will let her go, taking their two children to his mother's.

She will lay back against the seat of the taxi and say, 'I have never felt so free in all my life.'

Fady is a taxi driver who kindly befriended me. He and his wife Leila and their two girls, Pamela and Cindy, asked me to go with them on their annual holiday. It was an opportunity I couldn't pass up. We travelled in a convoy of three buses filled with Coptic Orthodox Christians on their annual vacation to the beach. The northern shores of Egypt are lined with condominiums and multi-story holiday flats housing millions of Egyptians escaping the Cairo heat.

I was the only foreigner on board. Travelling through the desert we visited several monasteries and at one stage we came to the Monastery of Saint Mena, the twelve-year-old boy who was martyred during Roman times. It was also where the resting place of the last Coptic Pope was displayed. Fady motioned me to pay homage and to pray at his tomb. I declined and stood back in respect, not quite comfortable with what was going on. I'm a Protestant and pray to Jesus, but my dear Orthodox friends have found other ways to God through the intercession of the saints as well as Jesus. (It has been explained to me since that when we ask a friend to pray for us, then we are doing the same. The Orthodox believers make use of the friends too, but they are with the Lord in the 'cloud of witnesses'.)

Later, on return home, I found out that Nevine had visited the same shrine a day or two after our visit. She had said a prayer for me and even pushed a piece of paper with the prayer written on it into the side of the glass coffin joining the hundreds of others. There was no way I was not going to be blessed – my Egyptian friends were determined.

Regarding my reasons for leaving the beach early, I couldn't tell Nevine that I just wanted to get home. I couldn't tell her that I couldn't bear another day with fifty million Egyptians bathing around the huge bay at Mersa Matruah. I couldn't tell her that the heat, and the noise and the endless gaze oppressed me - the male gaze.

I couldn't tell her that the four-deep umbrellas, clinging as a thick sward around the bay, oppressed me. And I not able to find Fady and family among the myriad of paddling, laughing, children. And the women, like full-blown peonies, sitting fully clothed in the shallow water eating sunflower seeds. And the thousands of other ladies dressed in bright synthetic dresses endlessly manoeuvring for the elusive shade. I wanted out!

Night Journeys

I wanted to get home to my flat in the Cairo suburb of 2 million souls, where the traffic never stopped, where the neighbours never slept and where the local mosque's call to prayer, five times a day, filled the air. Where I sought aural protection with my CD's on - earphones pressed close. To my home, where I could be alone, and not share my bed with others, and not sit at table spooning in tepid food and getting lost in the midday heat among the cheerful holidaying Egyptians!

The kindness of Fady and Leila suffocated me. I was ashamed that the individualism of my Australian culture was winning over the close communal living that was being offered me. I wanted escape. So I opted for the bus ride, and turned my back on the protection of friends.

By taking the public bus home I had put myself in moral danger. In the Muslim world-view I had placed temptation in the way of all those poor men on the bus! Women are responsible for *nine parts of desire*, as we are reminded in a book of that title.

But I knew that Fady had put some safe guards in place. He made sure that the bus driver knew that Fady had written his name down on the paper in his hand. Fady stood there and watched the men as they filed into the bus while I perched on that front seat, my swelling knee expanding inside my jeans. Fady noted the bus number and made sure that it was seen by all; that he had written it down on the paper he had put in his pocket. He had done his best, against my determination to return home two days early.

****

And as far as the taxi journey was concerned, my Egyptian women work colleagues only shook their heads in disbelief.

The men on staff weren't much impressed either: I had put the men on that bus in danger of losing merit because of their potential to lust!

Chapter Thirty Seven

Sabry and his Sisters
(July 1999)

My travelling days from Cyprus had finished. I finally had my home in Egypt. My dream to work on the editorial team of the youth magazine was being fulfilled. It had been an honour to travel so widely, recruiting personnel, and raising awareness of what Jesus was doing in the Middle East. But travelling just in Egypt would be adventurous enough.

And so I settled into my new apartment with Felicity, Mark, and Holly Joy, living directly across the corridor. This was a great joy to me and I remember some cute things that happened. One day Holly had a new dolly arrive in the post from England. When asked by her parents what she would like to call it, she said 'Diarrhoea.' Another time when they were over at my place having a curry, she declared, 'My dinner looks like poo.' Living in Egypt and being a toddler, such bodily functions were always cause for conversation and Holly Joy was quite the conversationalist. Holly May in Adelaide, South Australia was a great talker too – must be in the genes!

Felicity and I enjoyed recalling how we first met in India and then meeting up years later in Blackpool. Now we were neighbours in Cairo!

It really is a small world!

Sabry our landlord was a very amiable, tall, well-built man, his looks reflecting both his Egyptian and German heritage. He was in his thirties and appeared to enjoy his international tenants. The others who lived in that block had nothing but good things to say about him. Sabry had two sisters. The sisters, aged in their mid-twenties, occupied the fourth and the fifth floors and Sabry lived on the third floor.

Night Journeys

There was always lots of laughter and visiting going on between the international tenants. Once a month, on a Friday, all the tenants came to my flat for lunch after church. They would stay the afternoon and sometimes well into the night.

I had been in Sabry's apartment once to pay the rent and sign the lease. I found it book-lined and very business-like with modern dark wood furniture. Sabry and his sisters were well educated, having lived most of their lives with their mother in Hamburg, Germany. Their Egyptian father was a journalist who met his wife at university. Over the years, the children and their father came to Egypt for special occasions, usually when a family member had died or was getting married.

I remember a conversation with Sabry. He told me, 'We hate living in Egypt and we can't abide our Egyptian relatives so we never visit anyone and they don't visit us.'

'Then why are you here?' I asked.

'Our father died recently and left me this apartment house. I feel obliged to make something of my inheritance.'

'What about your mother?'

'We have no contact with her. She left our father. We are finished with her.'

'Then you are very close to your sisters?'

'Yes. We are all we have. They are my responsibility.'

For the entire time I lived there, just over twelve months, Sabry tried to make a garden. He would dig it up and fill it in, plant some trees and then tear them out again. Except for a row of ficus trees he grew like a hedge along the front fence to add privacy, nothing else took root. Sabry always appeared to be busy, putting up lights, taking them down, putting them up again; changing his mind.

On my first day there, I was introduced to an empty tiled pool-like feature in the front area. A possible pond, or a water- feature, or maybe even a lawn? Sabry had several ideas to improve the front. At that time the empty pool had an oblong shape and would have made a fun place for children to play, or if filled in, to grow a lawn. I read somewhere that in the whole of Cairo there was only a postage stamp size of green lawn for each citizen. This piece of lawn would have served a good purpose. But that too was dug up and filled in over and over again.

The same went for upgrading the apartment house; nothing was ever accomplished. Sabry never approached registered electricians, but hired men from the midan (round-a-bout) for any job needed. These men would stand behind their modest row of tools and wait for work each day. It always saddened me to see these men from out of town, sometimes with their young sons in tow, hoping for work. They would return to their families at night. I was impressed that Sabry used these men.

I was concerned when none of my lights worked after one of these men had worked on the wiring. A friend checked the wiring and found all the wires put in back to front.

Each day Sabry and his sisters went to the Sports Club and played tennis and squash for hours on end. Although they were secular, the girls wore the *hegab* around their heads. But that was the only concession to Muslim dress. They seemed to have no idea of what was culturally expected. The girls had their arms bare and wore shorts.

Sabry told me, 'We never walk to the Club any more. My sisters were verbally abused by men in the street. If I'm not there they leer at them and follow them home.'

Each morning they would disappear into the car. They were attractive girls but never engaged in conversation with me. Whenever we met on the stairs, they would smile sweetly and hurry up the stairs. I presumed they were very shy and possibly had no English or Arabic, and none of us spoke German.

One of the young mothers who lived in the apartment block for a three-month period tells a story of when she locked herself out of the flat with her baby asleep inside. She describes her feelings:

'I was beside myself with new mother terror and worry. I ran up to Sabry's flat and asked for help. He didn't have a spare key and couldn't force the door open so he went to the side of the building and climbed up to our bedroom balcony! He had to break through the French windows into the room where our baby was sleeping.

'As I thanked him – I was a bit tearful – he exclaimed over and over again what a good mother I was to care so much about my baby! He couldn't believe how much I loved him. It was very sweet, but made me a bit sad too as he was not at all connected to children. He was obviously touched by the whole incident. He was covered in dust from breaking in!'

Felicity told me that she thought Sabry appeared to be paranoid and fearful. 'I remember when a young man called Peter stayed in our apartment when we were away. Sabry was really worried about his potential behaviour. I had to announce, "Peter is a good Christian boy and won't be having girls to stay" for Sabry to back down.'

Felicity concluded: 'We felt his fear came more from utter bewilderment at trying to negotiate life. He didn't have good Arabic. His sisters never talked to me really, just muttered greetings. I don't remember their names.'

****

Sabry informed me early in my tenancy, 'My sisters are fashion designers. They will use the ground floor for a Show Room, so I am preparing the rooms for them.'

And, sure enough, pink marble greeted us each time we made our way across the foyer, past the fake lift and up the stairs. Sabry's sisters never got anywhere near their goal of starting a fashion house. The pink marble glowed softly like a promise unfulfilled on the foyer wall, with no one but to us tenants and our friends to appreciate it.

Sabry travelled for weeks at a time. Occasionally I would go to the girls' apartment to pay the rent when Sabry was away. They would not let me in. This was most unusual. Perhaps they had been told by their

Raylene Pearce

big brother not to let anyone in. I'd understand them being forbidden to allow a man to pass their threshold, but a woman?

Once, when I shoved a wad of Egyptian pounds through the slightly opened door, I got a glimpse of a barren room with one sewing machine against the wall.

Odd, I thought.

****

Where can I go from Thy Spirit?
Or where can I flee from Thy presence?
If I ascend to heaven, Thou art there;
If I make my bed in Sheol, behold, Thou art there.
If I dwell in the remotest part of the sea,
even there Thy hand will lay hold of me.
If I say, "Surely the darkness will overwhelm me,
and the light around me will be night",
Even the darkness is not dark to Thee,
And the night is as bright as the day.
Darkness and light are alike to Thee.

Psalm 139 V 7-12
New American Standard Bible, The Lockman Foundation,
La Habra, Calif. 1973

Chapter Thirty Eight

Invalid

I scrape the bowls of vegetable soup down the toilet, moaning, '*Mishma'ool, mishma'ool*'. 'Unbelievable'.

Then I slosh rice, salad, and bits of chicken into the bin in my tiny kitchen: a typical Egyptian kitchen. There is a little window which opens into the central well of the apartment block, letting in no light but funnelling loud shrieks, wailing music, cooking smells, dust and sand, and giving access, via the filthy walls and dangling electrical wiring, to visiting rats.

My language tutor, Amal, puts her head around the corner and hisses in English, 'Where is your Arabic?'

I fling the tea towel in the air. 'Why should I speak Arabic when none of you will speak to each other? Not a single word spoken the entire meal!'

'I spoke to Leila when we arrived and Joseph spoke to Reda.'

'But why not at the table?'

'We are not the same class. We don't have anything in common.'

'What? I picked you both to come together because you are Orthodox Christians, so you can talk about your church and … and … your priests!'

Amal did not reply, just shrugged her shoulders, and kindly asked if she could help serve the dessert. What could go wrong with fruit salad and ice cream? What indeed!

I had been living in an international community for six years. During that time, there were over thirty different nationalities represented at my table and I had never had my cooking refused. One night for example, I had two Malaysian nurses who worked in Afghanistan, a Dutch couple working in Syria, a Cypriot/Armenian woman whose family had been exterminated by the Turks and a BBC journalist who was covering the Middle East, all together at my table. They ate everything I cooked, and laughed and chatted throughout the meal.

Not tonight.

'What's this?' Reda screws up his nose and sniffs the soup.

'Soup,' I say. I can't think of the Arabic for soup although I had practised the vocab I thought I would need for the meal.

Then Leila sticks her fork into my beautifully fluffy, always appreciated, micro-waved rice, withdraws it, sniffs it, tastes it, makes a face and puts down her fork. Pamela and Cindy, named after American friends of theirs, watch and shadow their mother. So when she and Reda refuse the soup and the rice, so do the girls. Amal and Joseph and little Shams eat theirs, sitting at the far end of the table, too far from me to help me deal with these 'indignities'. They all eat the chicken bought from the local *souk*, so not all was a failure.

They appeared puzzled by the fruit salad, served with ice cream. I'm pleased to say they did eat that, but with an air of doing so to please me, rather than enjoying the food.

Later I found out that most Egyptians only eat food like their mothers cook. The rice is always cooked in oil on top of the stove and soup is only served when you are sick. And fruit salad is served in fruit-sized chunks, not neatly chopped up—that's for sick people too! And Reda and Leila's family never speak at meals. Meals are for eating. You speak later.

Reda and Leila didn't think the evening was a disaster. They were only puzzled because I gave them food for invalids!

They even said '*teslan ideeky*' which is a polite complement said after an enjoyable meal and meaning 'bless your hands'.

****

Night Journeys

From the fruit of their lips
people are filled with good things,
and the work of their hands brings them rewards.

Proverbs 12 v 14

****

Fayoum

'Raylene you're the meat in the sandwich!' shouted Betty from the back seat of the mini bus.

Wedged in with three others in a space usually reserved for two, I called back, 'No Betty, more like a slice of cheese.'

This melting slice of cheese and the others in my party tumbled out, only to be gathered up again for the next bus ride before boarding a converted truck to take us out to the lake.

Yes, a lake. A mystical place; with pink haze hovering above the tranquil water as the silent wash of ghostly fishing boats glide towards the centre.

In the shallows two Egyptian couples splashed each other amid screams of laughter. It's always a shock to my cultural expectations to see such joyous abandonment in a society like this. At heart I think Egyptians love fun, but usually restrict it to single sex activities in public.

We were visiting *Fayoum*, a major Oasis, two, and a half hours north east of Cairo. We travelled on six buses within the boundaries of this lush, heavily-planted-with-fruit-trees-and- glorious-multi-coloured-flowering-shrubs, Oasis. Date palms and bananas filled any space that might once have been open fields. This is close farming in the extreme.

Thomas was taking us to visit his Aunt Maryam, his mother's sister. We had afternoon tea with her and the family with a time of prayer together before reluctantly leaving. They had asked us to stay the night, as Egyptian hospitality knows no bounds. We needed to board two more buses before reaching home and could delay no longer.

One interesting fact of the prayer time was that we were instructed to face a particular direction. We were taken to a room that looked like a private sitting room with long windows. I found out later we were facing Jerusalem. We were shown the tattoo each family member had on the lower arm. Even two-year-old Mira had the tiny cross to signify her allegiance to Jesus. The Coptic cross forms a square representing the gospel going to the four corners of the earth. On the end of each arm of the cross is an ornate three-pointed flare indicating the Trinity.

We clambered on the bus loaded with sugar cane for chewing (the kids love it) and huge, hydrated dates twice the size of your middle finger.

****

Night Journeys

Sunflower in the Egyptian desert taken by James Winter

The desert and the parched land will be glad;
the wilderness will rejoice and blossom.
Like the crocus, it will burst into bloom;
it will rejoice greatly and shout for joy.
Then will the eyes of the blind be opened
and the ears of the deaf unstopped.
Then will the lame leap like a deer,
and the mute tongue shout for joy.
Water will gush forth in the wilderness
and streams in the desert.

Isaiah 35 v 1 - 2, 5 – 6

Chapter Thirty Nine

Women in Print (2000 - 2004)

One of my jobs on the editorial team was to collect personal stories from women. Here are a few to give you an idea of what it's like to be a modern young woman in Egypt – 2000. I think it is probably still the same now and in some cases more difficult.

As a single white female I resorted to wearing a wedding ring and lying regarding my status, so that I had some sort of peace traversing the streets, bazaars and train stations of Egypt. We advised our single girls to do the same, wear a wedding ring and that's usually enough, especially needed for the fair hair, fair skin girls.

Night Journeys

Unmarried in Egypt

'Yesterday I turned thirty-seven years old and I'm still not married! But it's not my problem. It's my mother's!' Mira sighs into her tea as she continues. 'She's at me day and night: "Why are you not married? Will I ever see my grandchildren? What if I die before you are married? Will I ever see you dressed in white on the arm of your husband?" She makes me feel abnormal and unlovely. And I know I'm neither.'

The group of friends complete their lunch together in a local café and I join them for coffee. Two of them who are married run off to be home in time for their children after school. So Iman stays on sympathising with her friend Mira and chatting to me about the bumpy life of a single thirty-something, living in Egypt and having to put up with all the nonsense that is thrown at you.

Refrains like: 'What is wrong with you? Don't you like men? Don't men like you? Perhaps if you change your hair, lose weight … On and on it goes.'

Mira adds how her mother had set her up to meet this man who was fifty years old, a widow with two kids.

'I'm supposed to be the next wife to a man as old as my own father—what sort of life would that be? Can't he find someone his own age?' She groans into a fresh cup of coffee.

Warming to her subject Mira continues, 'What's wrong with men that they can't pick a bride from their own generation? What has a man of fifty got to say to an educated woman of thirty? I suppose he can talk about the first twenty years of his life before she was born … if she's interested in ancient history! Or the following ten years while he was in his first job and she still at school—how boring is that?'

Iman turns to me, 'A major problem is the bad economic times. It's still the custom for the boy to have a flat ready in time for marriage. Now the boys are becoming grown men in their late thirties and early forties and the girls are growing into women in their mid thirties—and are still not married! Then the men in their late thirties get it into their heads to marry girls in their early twenties, sometimes fifteen years their junior.'

'So where does that leave girls like you?' I ask, 'Although these days women can have children in their late thirties and early forties.'

Mira and Iman give me a 'look' through their long thick eyelashes. 'Girls today want more out of marriage than having children and cooking meals for their husbands,' Iman says.

'They want someone who can share their lives, can talk about subjects that interest them—someone who at least has lived through the same world events and can recall similar experiences.'

I agree, and Mira takes it up. 'I have a friend who has no mother or father and no uncles and aunts but an older brother who is continually onto her to marry. She is thirty-eight and he is nearly forty and wants to marry. He feels he cannot until she is safely cared for, but she just hasn't met anyone she feels she can spend the rest of her life with. She's in a dilemma. What is the answer for her?

'I know she would love to share the rent and live in a flat with a number of respectable single girls and take away the responsibility from her brother. But no one in our society allows such freedom. They suspect any girls who aren't under their father or husband's protection. We are in the twenty-first century. Sometimes I feel like I am living in the middle ages, or in Jane Austen's time.'

We all sigh, think of Mr Darcy, and I order more coffee and the biggest chocolate cakes in the shop.

****

The Other Side of the Coin

Maryam is very attractive; the sort of woman who makes both men, and women, turn their heads in admiration. She has large brown eyes that twinkle as she speaks, a modern hairstyle cut to the nape of her neck and stylish clothes. She is an evangelical Christian, educated, an Egyptian thirty-something confident woman, single and satisfied.

Why?

I asked Maryam to share her thoughts on the 'being single' question. She wrote this out and I share it with you now:

I have no home responsibilities. I love mother's cooking and she loves to cook for us. I love to help my mother, but it's not my major concern, like it is for her. I can go in and out without asking my husband's permission and I can change plans whenever I want to. A mobile phone call to my mother keeps me connected but not chained.

Without kids I can travel for many days and stay overnight with friends. I can attend conferences for work in other cities. I am more open to meeting new people and making new friends than most married women. I have complete freedom to choose my own clothes and hairstyle.

Looking back over the 30 years of my life I have no regrets because I have been able to travel overseas and have had other positive experiences. I have become independent and can do things like dealing with government offices' paper-work, buying heavy equipment or electronic gear by myself.

I can pursue a career with the possibility of promotion into a management position with international connections. I have the freedom to work longer hours that is prohibitive for married women who have other responsibilities. I have been able to concentrate on further education possibilities and read whatever and whenever I like.

I love to go to the theatre and to concerts and shop for new clothes without feeling guilty that I should be using the money to buy the children's shoes, for example. I delight in buying toys and clothes for my nieces and nephews, so I'm not missing out on that. I love being an Aunt.

If you are single and satisfied you can be a great resource for your other single friends who might be unhappy for one reason or the other, or maybe widowed or divorced. I know I have been able to encourage them because I know what it is at times to feel lonely, but also know how to live an abundant life – without a husband!

Remember you are still alive and tomorrow may be the beginning of something or someone new in your life.

Jesus said, 'Do not worry about tomorrow, for tomorrow will worry about itself.'

So don't worry about being in your thirties and single. Enjoy today, live it to the full, serve others, care for those who are struggling, look forward to the days of your life as a gift from God and He will bless you.

If you cannot enjoy life as a single – you cannot expect to enjoy life as a married.

****

Sabrya's Dilemma

'I signed the paper. It said we were married and now I'm trapped. I dare not tell my parents. They will kill me. What shall I do? I can't pray to God. I'll kill myself. That's what I'll do!'

The desperate girl, eyes staring out of her headscarf, grasped Sonya's arm. Could she trust this woman? Sabrya has watched her for two weeks. She bought the magazine. She read it. She had absorbed the integrity and hope in its pages. It spoke of the family, of love, relationships, and marriage. She had to trust this woman. There was no one else. She couldn't share her awful secret with her friends.

So they meet outside the imposing university gates that guard 70,000 girls coming from all over the Arab world. Sabrya continues, 'I know "my husband" wants to escape from this "marriage". I feel this and I will be alone. What shall I do?'

Sonya looks at the frightened nineteen year old girl and says, 'We'll pray to God to get this idea of killing yourself out of your mind. God is still you Father.' As she says this Sabrya's eyes fill up as she grasps hold of this wonderful truth. 'If you ask God to forgive you, He will. And we'll ask him to heal you and provide a way out of your troubles.'

Sonya, an attractive woman in her early 40's, is a Christian and works for a youth magazine that is circulated each month through newsstands in 15 countries throughout the Middle East and North Africa. Several times a year Sonya gets permission to sell it in universities. For this assignment Sonya wears the conservative Muslim dress to be allowed into the grounds.

She knows that Sabrya is not alone with the problem of 'secret marriages'. A Muslim man can go to the mosque and buy a certificate of marriage signed by the mullah. They present it to the girl they desire and she is tricked into a sexual relationship. This is not a proper marriage. Sometimes it is issued for one night only! Many young women are caught up in it with no one to turn to when they are dropped, as eventually they will be, because Muslim men will only marry virgins.

It is Sonya's experience that when Muslim women get as desperate as this, they call out to God, as Father. It is a belief not taught at this great university. By reading the magazine girls discover that God is a loving God. The magazine seems to touch their hearts and draw them close to Him.

****

Confessions of a Wife

I have always dreamed of a happy home in which happiness glows and the sun of love warms it.

I confess that many times I imagined myself as a lady in a big palace full of the most exquisite furniture and rare antiques. My dream came true and exceeded my imagination. I got married right after I graduated from high school, as it was the tradition in my family. My husband was rich. He satisfied my desire for possessions. He didn't hesitate to fulfil my numerous needs that satisfied my ostentatious love. I don't deny my husband was loving, and tender. I lived with him the most beautiful years of my life. I have always felt pity for my friends who didn't experience happiness in their marriage and ended up divorced. I didn't know anything about divorce.

Many times I wondered, 'Why do people marry today and divorce tomorrow? How is a divorcee to go on with her life and accept the failure every day as people look at her?

'Is not there anyone who can guarantee her honour?'

I never imagined that one day I would be going through this experience. Happiness that filled every corner in our house started to disappear because my husband was busy at work and I was busy feeling pity. We couldn't understand each other anymore and disagreements and fights broke out. The shock was horrible when my husband divorced me five years later. I surrendered to feelings of hatred, bitterness, and anger. Those detestable feelings took over and made me hate, envy and seek revenge for myself. I couldn't imagine that I hated the man I loved years before. I tried over and over to restore the feeling of dignity and turn over a new leaf in my life, but the eruption deep within and bitterness would show on my face.

I remember the day my life changed. God touched the depth of my wound and healed me. I was reading the Bible that a friend gave me. Tears ran down my cheeks when I found my heart crying out with the same words the prophet David prayed in Psalm 6:

> *'O Lord, do not rebuke me in your anger*
> *or discipline me in your wrath.*
> *Be merciful to me for I am faint;*
> *O LORD, heal me, for my bones are in agony.*
> *My soul is in anguish…deliver me;*
> *save me because of your unfailing love…*

Night Journeys

I am worn out from groaning;
all night I flood my bed with weeping
and drench my couch with tears.'

These words were like a spring flowing within me. Then I read the promise that put my heart at ease:

'…..and call upon me in the day of trouble;
I will deliver you, and you will honour me.' Psalm 50:15

The promise that brought shining light into my life again is:

'If we confess our sins he is faithful and just and will forgive us our sins and purify from all unrighteousness.' 1 John 1:9

I felt a new person. I prayed to God, saying, 'I confess my sins. I confess that I am holding on to everything that is transient. My hatred and malice expose me. I am unable to help myself and unite with my family. I cast everything before you in order for you to cleanse and purify me and make me whole again.'

God answered my prayer and brought my husband back. He and I have a living relationship with God and enjoy a happy life based on the divine love, which forgives and is not easily provoked and doesn't think evil, that love which never fails, and no man can destroy.

****

Chapter Forty

Mentioning More Men

Hani is a friend of mine.

While he was fixing my computer he told me this story:

Hani had a computer business, where among other things he did, he trained people. One day a young woman came for lessons.

After some weeks he said to her, 'I know someone who would make you a good husband.'

She said, 'Don't talk to me.'

Later he repeated himself, and she said, 'Don't talk to me. It's none of your business.'

He said, 'It is my business. The person I am talking about is me.'

She said, 'Don't say another word. Speak to my brother or father.' And raced from the room.

Hani had seen Maie at church but it wasn't till he began to teach her that he had come to love her. So he went to her brother. The brother took him to Maie's father.

Hani said, 'I have a flat, a car (not too good but it goes) and a business (that is going fairly well). I want to marry your daughter.'

The father said, 'Is this an emotional attachment?'

Hani replied, 'I love your daughter.'

Maie's father said, 'You cannot base a marriage on emotional attachment. You cannot marry my daughter.'

Some months went by and things changed in Hani's life. His own father's business collapsed and Hani sold his flat and gave his father the money. Hani's own business started to deteriorate but his old car kept chugging on.

Undaunted, he approached Maie's father again.

'I no longer have a flat. My business is not doing so well but I still want to marry your daughter.'
  Maie's father's said, 'You had a flat before, what happened to it?'
'I sold it.'
'Why did you sell it?'
'My father needed the money.'
'Why did you give him the money?'
'Because he is my father.'
Then Maie's father said, 'You can marry my daughter.'
  After the proposal was accepted, Hani's father's business improved and an Uncle (his father's brother) presented Hani with a flat!

At the time Hani told me his story, they have been married a year, and Maie was expecting their little boy in three months time.
  The car still chugs on.

****

Also, during the time I was English Language Editor I collected stories to be used for the theme of each month.

Theme 1

Being young and capable: How to cope with pressure.

A Bedouin man from the White Desert told these two stories.
  Maher was only 17. One morning his father let him drive the 4WD Toyota Land-cruiser into the desert taking a short cut off the road, through the sands, to his grandmother's village.
  Not long into the trip a sandstorm overtook him. He kept driving. He knew this was important for his survival. But the sandstorm was huge and soon he lost his bearings. The air surrounding him was deep

orange and the sun was blocked out. Soon it became dark and he had no idea in what direction he was travelling. So he stopped the car, and tried to keep out the sand that seeped into the vehicle like sieved rice.

Grabbing a bottle of water, Maher put a blanket over his head and curled up on the front seat to wait out the storm.

The storm raged for four days and nights. The great Sahara was shifting in the power of the winds. Maher coped by sipping the water, conserving his energy, and never giving up hope.

Many years later, when Maher confirmed his story we asked him if he thought he was going to die.

'Never,' he said. 'To think that way is the sure way to die. You must cope under pressure and never give up hope. My father taught me the skills of surviving in the desert and I did what he told me.

'After five days, I dug my way out of the car. The air was still and the colour of pale orange, but the sun was still hidden. So I sat in the car and waited. As the air began to clear I could make out the soft light of the sun. Then I was able to work out the direction back to my village. So I started to walk, following the setting sun, knowing that we would return to bring the car back later.

'There was a great party to celebrate my survival in the desert. My whole family thought I had died there, but not my father. He knew what he had taught me and he trusted me that I would follow his teachings and cope.'

Iron is put under pressure to strengthen it. Likewise, Maher became strong.

****

Night Journeys

Theme 2

Desert Rescue: What is just and fair?

The old Bedouin moved the wood into the centre of the fire and continued his story.

'Last year one of our guides took five Japanese tourists into the Sahara for a two day trip. After four days the Japanese Embassy started to get worried and sent people into our village.

'We had this boy. He was only 12 years old, but he had a special gift for finding people lost in the desert. We took him to the last place that we had searched for the lost tourists and he gazed about him.

'"Have you looked in that valley?" the boy asked, pointing to a depression on the horizon where we had not yet been.

'"No," we said.

'"Then look there. It is where you will find the Japanese."

'So we went in that direction and we soon found the five Japanese who were almost unconscious, and we brought them back to the village. An ambulance, organised by the Embassy, took them to the city for treatment.

'The villagers asked us, "Where is the driver?"

'To our horror we realised we hadn't found him.'

'"Never mind," they said. "He'll be dead by now. Leave him."

'"No," I said, "that's not fair," and with my elder son we set out once more, without even a rest, to search for the old driver. Praise God we found him, just in time, and raced him to our local hospital.

****

'On the way the police stopped us and tried to arrest him for causing the Japanese tourists so much trouble.

'I said to the policemen, "Are five Japanese tourists more important than one old man? Tell me, is it just that he should die?"

'So they let us go. At top speed we raced to the hospital where salt water and honey drink was waiting to revive our old Bedouin guide.'

****

> He has shown you, O man, what is good.
> And what does the LORD require of you?
> To act justly and to love mercy
> and to walk humbly with your God.

Micah 6 v 8

****

Chapter Forty One

Eid el Adha

On the feast of Eid el Adha I'd stay at home. I wouldn't even look out of my window for fear of seeing an animal's throat cut. The blood collected in a bowl and a family, delighting in scooping up the still warm, once living fluid, smearing it on themselves and then on everything in sight.

Some weeks before the Feast of Sacrifice a cow was coaxed, rather roughly, up our staircase. We had seven floors in the block I lived in. That meant fourteen landings where the poor doomed beast was allowed to pause in its ascent to its killing ground – the roof. For several weeks the beast was fattened up, and seventy days after Ramadan my neighbours, along with all the Muslim world, celebrated the Feast of Sacrifice.

The Feast started with the usual Call to Prayer from all the mosques of Cairo at about 4.30a.m. The faithful would proceed to the nearest mosque, or like my neighbours over the corridor they'd all wake, ceremonially wash their face and hands and kneel on their prayer mats. Mahmoud, the father, leading the prayers. Then the children would pile back into bed to sleep for another couple of hours.

Sometime during the morning the butcher arrived. The family assembled on the roof to watch Mahmoud hold the cow's head. Mohammad, the first-born son, would rest his hand on the knife as the butcher made a clean cut of the jugular artery and the blood caught in a bowl. All the family would be anointed and the blood splashed all around the building.

When I finally left my apartment a stream of blood would be congealing on the stairs, making it impossible to avoid getting it on the soles of my shoes. Along the corridor, handprints of blood, like a macabre wallpaper, patterned each surface, including the doors. Outside, the butchers in their donkey carts, piled high with the skins of the sacrificed animals, called out for any more customers. Blood-painted buses and taxis congested the streets.

On that day the poor would be fed meat, a portion always given away from each animal. I was included in that as I was invited to share a meal that Eid with my neighbours. Hanan used every part of the animal and made huge sausages from the intestine skin. We'd sit at a small table covered in newspaper and eat our hearts out – I'll leave you to imagine the rest.

Most of my Muslim friends weren't too clear what it was all about. I seemed to know more about their religion than they did, and they did get a number of major things wrong about this Feast. This Feast is in remembrance of when Abraham took Ishmael to Mount Moriah, to sacrifice him upon an altar. Then Allah provided a sheep to be killed in his place and so the people celebrate every year this wonderful story of God's provision of an animal sacrifice. They do it year after year after year, just like the Jews did on the Day of Atonement in Jesus' day ... and still do today.

Not only do these dear people misunderstand what is happening, but they have Abraham going up the mountain with the wrong son!

Isaac, the 'child of promise' was the one who was to be sacrificed as a foreshadowing of Jesus' sacrifice. In the first case a ram is given so the boy is free, but people who still insist in acting out this story have missed the point.

The point is an everlasting outcome, not ever to be repeated. Jesus, the Lamb of God, offered himself as an unblemished sacrifice. He, sacrificed on a Roman cross, absorbed all the sin of the world for all time at an appointed time in God's eternal plan. He did that by dying and rising from the dead, so defeating death itself! Then ascending to the Father and sending the Holy Spirit so that we are now free from all those dead-end efforts to please God. And one day he will return and those who believe in Jesus will inherit the new heaven and the new earth!

The last words in the Bible are, in Rev 22 v 20, 21: Come, Lord Jesus. And then a blessing: The grace of the Lord Jesus Christ be with God's people. Amen.

The people of Islam are stuck! They progress no further in their understanding of God's perfect sacrifice through this feast. They are forever trapped on a treadmill of doing good deeds to satisfy an insatiable god.

The sad thing is that we too can get on the treadmill of doing good deeds to please God. We easily forget it is by grace we have been saved, not from anything we might do – whether it's coming to church, being on a committee, doing good works, or just being a generous person.

We must not live as people who lived before the perfect sacrifice. We live under the New Covenant. We share in the work of the Body of Christ, as a grateful response for what Jesus has done for us.

****

For it is by grace you have been saved, through faith -
and this is not from yourselves, it is the gift of God -
not by works, so that no one can boast.

Ephesians 2 v 8 & 9

Night visit to Shoubra

Shoubra is one of the older areas of Cairo with buildings piling on top of each other in a glorious muddle of millions of people living out their lives close together.

Stephanie, a colleague from England who has given her life for the people of this nation, is taking me to her part of the city. From our work place we have taken the tube, changed trains, and now walk through narrow sandy streets.

It's the cool of the evening and the place is fully alive. Stalls fill every space carrying all kinds of wares - fruit and veg, ladies' nighties and fish. The streets are filled with people of all ages looking, walking, talking, buying, and selling. What a buzz. You get the definite impression that these people are very connected.

This photo is not from Shoubra but it does give an idea of how close Egyptian people like to live.

Stephanie has chosen to live in this highly populated area so that she can become part of the unique community of Shoubra. Although there are somewhere up to 6 million people living in this district, there's a feeling of connection that I don't think we experience anymore in the West. There's so little privacy in Shoubra and I've a feeling that most people know each others' business and that seems to be OK with them.

This week is the Coptic Orthodox Feast of the Virgin Mary and Shoubra has a high percentage of Christians living there. As we make our way through the bazaar, hanging overhead and in many windows are lit-up crosses and pictures of Mary and the infant Jesus. Further down the street we see flashing coloured lights and highly decorated tents filled with boxes of sweets to celebrate the Prophet's birthday! Both 'moveable' feasts, this year, are in the same week. So people live side by side and buy and sell, both Muslim and Christian respecting each person's beliefs. This busy picture will continue to all hours of the morning.

Stephanie lives 9 floors up, on the roof in fact. After climbing those dark, narrow stairs you wouldn't like to have to make a quick trip down to pick up a lost bit of laundry or forgotten grocery item. There's no lift!

The view is breathtaking. Whole communities of people live on the rooftops, and I spent ages just gazing out over the tightly packed buildings. Perving would have been another name for it!

In one window a mother feeds her baby. A colourful rug is beaten from another. Washing flaps in the breeze. A man fashions cushions, carefully sewing.

We eat out on the roof as the sun slowly slips behind the pink haze that blankets the city. My nose reacts to the everlasting pollution so that I have to take anti-histamines day and night. I'm fit at the moment, but I wouldn't like to climb nine flights of stairs each afternoon in the heat of summer.

I was a colleague of Stephanie's for ten years. She has continued to live in her tiny penthouse in Shoubra, and work for a Christian Egyptian NGO, which provides the poor with the dignity of start-up funds for their own businesses. This NGO provides education for children, literacy for adults and training and equipping in agricultural, health, youth and women's work.

The Kola Project has arisen out of this organisation bringing piped water into homes, and a future and a hope in Jesus Christ into their lives.
www.thinkanddo.org

****

Why support the Kola Project?

Excerpt from a talk by the author for International Day of Prayer 2014.

The sun was speaking to her, reminding her it was time to go for water. She did this every day so she made her way out of the village, the empty weight of the kola balanced easily on her head. Her bangles clinked and her bare feet trod the well-worn path. She was almost there.

Photo of a kola taken by Norm Tucker

She saw something move on her right side, a flash of colour. Then it was gone. She continued on her way. At the row of date palms she stopped, expecting the others to be there. Leila put down the kola and adjusted her hegab. They're probably there already, she thought, and hoisted the kola back on top of her head and proceeded to the water's edge.

No one there! No girlish chatter and laughter. Deserted. Strange. The flash again, but this time on her left. Before she had time to think about her situation they were upon her.

Leila never knew how many, or who they were. Probably boys from the village up stream. They punched her face and stomach, and ripped her clothes and stuffed her scarf in her mouth, choking any scream she could have made. She might have died there and then, had not the other girls arrived, and screaming and screaming and screaming they ran back the way they had come.

Photo by Greig Kidman of girls washing the family's clothes and dishes.

Leila would have remembered little of the first days. The immense pain, like she'd been torn in two, engulfed her. She was surrounded by the shrill of wailing, like a thick shroud draped over her. Lots of wailing. All her mother's friends and their relatives pressing in, filling the only room in Leila's house with wailing. Wailing over the ruin of a daughter. Wailing over the disgrace of a daughter. Wailing over the shame of an entire family.

Who would marry her now?

Abuna Thomas made his way through the crowd to the distraught family. He took Leila's broken hand and gently spoke to her of how the heart of Jesus was breaking to see his daughter so injured. He prayed words of comfort, and anointed her torn head with oil and wept as he gently poured holy water over her dying body.

****

Leila's village is in Upper Egypt nestled close to the Nile. The people no longer fear the annual flood that used to take them all away. But another fear has taken hold of them. The young girls, the water-carriers, have become targets for predatory youths.

In the early 2,000's, while I was living in Egypt, reports came through from Upper Egypt that Christian girls were being raped as they ventured near the Nile to wash clothes, dishes, the household animals, and carry water back to their homes.

The local authorities were unable to stop the attacks. It was evident that a creative intervention was needed. If it were too dangerous for the girls to go to the river, then the river would go to them.

Photo taken by Norm Tucker.

Leila died before the running water was piped into her house.

Leila died before a ceramic washbasin with a single tap and a plug, with ceramic tiles at the back, was attached to the dung coloured wall of the single room of Leila's parents' house.

No girl from this household would ever have to go to the Nile again to carry the family's supply of water. Now all they had to do was to turn on the tap! And they had a toilet too! This reduced the danger even more.

Also, they were no longer in danger of getting bilharzia, a parasite that burrows into the skin causing severe chronic illness.

Importantly, now there is more time in the day for the girls to attend school.

Photo taken by Greig Kidman of a girl beside a newly installed sink and tap.

This project also allows us, as readers, to move from being spectators of these stories to becoming participators in the lives of some poor families depicted in this book. Young girls are at risk until the money comes in, the whole amount must be received before one home can have the pipes installed.

On the back page are instructions on how this can happen.

****

The LORD will guide you always;
he will satisfy your needs
in a sun-scorched land
and will strengthen your frame.
You will be like a well-watered garden,
like a spring whose waters never fail.
Your people will rebuild the ancient ruins
and will be called Repairer of Broken Walls,
Restorer of Streets with Dwellings.

Isaiah 58 v 11 & 12

Chapter Forty Two

The Tale of Two Theatres (2000)

Let me tell you about the time I went to the movies in downtown Cairo with my language class. We were eight women from Korea, Costa Rica, Brazil, Uruguay, Egypt, and Australia, and all admirers of Mel Gibson.

We went to sigh over Mel's cheeky grin. But the movie we saw was 'Signs' and if you have seen it, you will remember that smiles are few and far between. Mel plays an Anglican priest who has lost his faith after the horrific death of his beloved wife. Not only is he working through this issue, he is fighting off belligerent aliens from outer space!

There was not much time for him to give us women a smile. But that didn't worry the audience. They were talking loudly to each other throughout, and reading the subtitles, getting up, going out, coming back, answering and talking loudly on their mobiles, crunching on assorted sweets and downing popcorn by the bucket.

They reminded me of going to the matinee on a Saturday afternoon when I was a kid—without the mobiles and the subtitles. The noise, as shrill as crickets cavorting in the evening, was a stand-out experience in going to the movies in this country, this city, in fact anywhere in this area of the world.

****

Raylene Pearce

Another Time, Another Movie
(2004)

After attending Palm Sunday service on Friday in one church, then attending another on Saturday in another, a small group of us expatriates went to the 10pm performance of Mel Gibson's film *The Passion of the Christ*.

We had a sense of history and a feeling of apprehension as we had all been to movies in this city before and wondered what the reception would be, what the noise level would be, and how much distraction there'd be.

We arrived at the Ramses Hilton Multiplex, theatre No 3, next door to No 2 where Tom Cruise in *The Last Samurai* was showing. We still couldn't quite believe it as we gazed at the posters advertising *The Passion of the Christ*. We entered the dimly lit theatre which was already half full and sat quietly while the rest of the audience did the same.

Once the movie began, the silence continued. Twice, a mobile phone rang but was cut off by the owner with no usual chat. No one was eating popcorn and no one read out the subtitles. In front of us was a row of people, their women wearing the higab. These folk, dotted around the theatre for whatever reason they were there, were being confronted with a story unlike any they had been taught before.

Then the interval. We expected everyone to get up and start for the doors to get drinks and popcorn. No one moved. A young man in the row in front of ours turned to Steve sitting beside me and said, 'I've seen this film five times. Each time I bring more friends with me. We are amazed.' At that Steve stood up and the two men had a muted conversation while the rest of us prayed or spoke to the people around us. The murmurs died down as the curtains parted and the final part of *The Passion of the Christ* presented itself to the captive audience.

Night Journeys

This film was allowed into Egypt because the powers thought it would stir up anti-Semitism. To facilitate this they allowed an extra copy of the film in, and theatres throughout Egypt showed continual screenings of the last hours of Jesus's earthly life for many weeks.

The final scene of the resurrection sealed it for many.

The head of the Bible Society said, 'This film has created a paradigm shift in how people view Jesus and the Gospel. It is nothing short of a miracle.'

In one of the local papers a young man, his name given, said in response to seeing the film, 'It's inspiring, and it makes you think about things that are against our beliefs but still somehow make sense.'

We all thought God had a great sense of humour, using a fallible Hollywood actor to break down century old barriers. To cause governments to change the law to allow a prophet's face to be shown. And in our case in Egypt to cause the law to be completely ignored!

A few weeks ago on my Chief Editor's desk was a sixteen-page insert from an ordinary secular newspaper regularly sold on the streets: sixteen pages filled with colour stills from the movie, scripture verses and discussions by church leaders. It was utterly amazing.

Whatever your own experience of this film has been in the West, to sit in the Ramses Hilton Multiplex No 3 on the banks of the Nile, in downtown Cairo, and watch the death and resurrection of the Christ with an engrossed audience of local people, has been the highlight of my ten years in the Middle East.

To be able to pray for these young people as they listened intently to the native language of Jesus, so like Arabic; to watch as the wrong idea that Christianity is somehow Western was thrown down. To see my own magazine out there on the newsstands with four-colour pages as a review of the film is nothing short of a work of God. To know that hundreds of young adult Christians handed out Skinny Luke's in Arabic, at cinemas all over Egypt was another miracle that God ordained.

In my personal experience, I feel that I have received a level of understanding for the first time in visual form of 'The Lamb of God who takes away the sin of the world'. As Jesus was lifted up on the cross, a close-up of his whip-scarred, red-striped torso filled the screen. He looked just like the lambs that had been slaughtered and hung up in front of the local butchers in my street!

I was able to feel with Mary as her son fell beneath the weight of the cross, as he says to her, 'See, I make all things new.' They lived together for thirty years! What did they talk about? It sent me back to the source material. What was it that the angel told the young Mary? What had she held in her heart? What warning had she had of a sword that would pierce her heart?

The movie spoke to Muslims with special power at this point. Mary, whom they revere, recognised her own son taken down from the cross. There is an Arab saying, 'Every woman knows her own son.' Muslims are taught that Jesus did not die on the cross, but an imposter was crucified instead. In the movie, Mary knows her son and that clinched it for many people. A stumbling block was being replaced by a foundation stone.

These are images that have created in me a greater appreciation of what Jesus went through. My sin put him there, along with Mel's and the rest of the world's!

****

> You see, at just the right time,
> when we were still powerless,
> Christ died for the ungodly.
> Very rarely will anyone die for a righteous man,
> though for a good man someone might possibly dare to die.
> But God demonstrates his own love for us in this:
> while we were still sinners,
> Christ died for us.
>
> Romans 5 v 8

Chapter Forty Three

Holy, Holy, Holy
Holy Water

It is the week after Coptic Christmas. Mercy asks me to celebrate the great feast, *The Feast of Saint John the Baptist's Baptism of Jesus,* with her and her brother Mikael. They meet me at the metro station and we walk through the *souk*, filled with stalls of fruit and vegetables, hanging carcases, rows of brassieres dangling above our heads, sandals and children's clothes, and flat bread on flat trays on young boy's heads, lit by twinkling coloured lights. The sand streets are narrow enough for people to talk to each other from window to window.

The ancient church of Raphael the Archangel is nearby behind a high mud wall: the bell tower is lit up with a cross as always, and now with a bright Christmas star. We enter the large courtyard filled with joyful people of all ages. We move into the packed church and Mercy finds a seat for us near the back among the women.

Mikael has disappeared with his friends. I have my *St Basil Liturgy* with me, written in Copt, Arabic and English, so that I can follow the service. It will go for four hours and I doubt that I will be able to stay the whole time.

Mercy and her girlfriends have had their hair styled for the festival, mainly in long curls loping down their shoulder blades. Each teenager wears a new dress and perfect makeup. Their profiles are seen on frescoed temple walls. It is the Christians of this land who are the ancient people, the descendants of the Pharaohs.

I had no idea this festival was so important. Easter is the biggest festival of the year, and now all the Coptic Christians of Egypt are celebrating the Festival of Saint John the Baptist's baptism of Jesus.

The Archangel Raphael's church is overflowing. The ceremony of the blessing of the water, where the parishioners place bottles of water under the altar to be made holy, takes about half an hour of prayers, chants and the swinging of incense. Later Father Philipos walks up and down the aisles carrying a blue plastic jug and, flaying an ornate brush, he splashes us all with water. The plastic blue jug fascinates me as the ordinary aligns with the ornate.

It is a joyful time. The priest's eyes gleam and the girls squeal as the water splatters their new curls. After the service Father Philipos tells me that he picks the girl with the fanciest hairstyle to give an extra dollop of water to.

What impresses me about the Coptic Church is that a sense of humour and fun are present, especially in happy occasions such as this one. This explains Father Philipos's pleasure in the girl's hair. He's a family man himself. Jesus must approve – he knows what the joy of life is all about – it's his gift: Love, JOY, peace … the fruit of the Spirit of God.

In his baptism Jesus joins himself with sinful humanity, going through the water as in death, and coming out of the water - raising us up with him - to life. When the voice from heaven says, 'You are my own dear Son,' Jesus shares his son-ship with those who are now joined to him, through their baptism.

A very good reason for the church's celebration!

I end up staying the whole service and love every minute, getting a second dousing of water after the sermon, almost three hours later, twice blessed.

****

While on the metro station waiting for the last train from Cairo to arrive, a tiny, bent-over woman shuffles by and sits beside me. She clutches her bottle of *Baraka*, newly blessed.

Night Journeys

(*Baraka* is Arabic for blessing and the trade name on the spring water bottles.)

She tells me she is taking it home to her sick old mother for her to drink and be healed.

> Since my youth, God, you have taught me
> and to this day I declare your marvellous deeds.
> Even when I am old and grey, do not forsake me, my God,
> till I declare your power to the next generation,
> your mighty acts to all who are to come.
> Your righteousness, God, reaches to the skies.
>
> Psalm 71 v 17-18

****

Holy Man

It took ages for the guards to search through the thick wad of my passport. They flipped the cover, turning it sideways to view my ageless photo. They peered at me in the half-light, back and forth, back and forth, making sure I really was whom I purported to be. Finally they let me in.

Mary was waved through, being Egyptian. But me, being a *farengi*, a foreigner, meant that they had to be really sure. Sure about what, I'm not sure. I don't think I looked like a terrorist, but these days you couldn't be too careful. One thing I have learnt living in the Middle East is that patience is an essential virtue, and I learnt fast.

I was going to see His Holiness Pope Shenouda the III, 117th Pope of Alexandria, the Patriarch of the See of St Mark and the head of the ancient Coptic Church of Egypt.

Raylene Pearce

I was being admitted into the immense womb of the new cathedral in Abbasiya, the high dome and bell tower silhouetted against the Cairo sky. It fought for space alongside the thousands of minarets and mosques, characteristic of the great city.

Carried along by the throng, I passed through the huge studded wooden doors, inlaid with Coptic crosses of mother-of-pearl and camel bone. I caught up with Mary, waiting patiently inside. She led me to a section near the front set aside for *farengu*. Along with several thousand people pressed in and overflowing the famous cathedral, we waited for the Pope's arrival.

Mary, a work colleague and devout Christian, had wanted to bring me to this famous weekly audience for some months. Wednesday night at the cathedral was the night the Pope graciously met his people.

Night Journeys

Amazed I watched hundreds of young people flocking towards the Cathedral grounds, to sit and chat on the lawns, getting into circles and groups. There was such a buzz of excitement – they were going to meet the Patriarch of their church! It felt like something else – young people waiting for their idol, their rock star, their football star to appear. Egyptian youth can get very excited at a football match or in a theatre when a James Bond movie is showing. But this was for a spiritual leader! I was assigned a lovely Coptic Nun to translate for me.

An hour of vibrant Coptic worship opened the proceedings, with rows of monks and priests moving slowly in procession to the front rows. The monks were dressed in their close black caps with Coptic crosses embroidered in gold thread on the forehead, at the ears and the centre back, over the brain stem. This is to signify that what they hear and think is covered by the cross of Christ. Each monk, answering the call of God on his life, enters a monastery after he has completed his tertiary education. Then, equipped with his degree, he tests his vocation as a celibate monk.

Depending on his gifts and motivation he will move through the ranks of the various orders in the monasteries in the great deserts of Egypt. Should he become a bishop, he will lead a major section of the ten million plus Coptic Christians in Egypt. Popes have been elected continuously from within the community of bishops since St Mark was head of the church in Egypt. Pope Shenouda was the 117th Pope.

The priests bringing up the procession, grand in their round high hats, all dressed in black, are married and live with their families within their parishes.

This minority group is often overlooked within the global community who see Egypt as a Muslim country only. The Copts originate from the ancient Egyptians and are not Arabs.

That evening the Pope gave a teaching, which I can still remember, about the love between David and Jonathan. He instructed his flock on the love that they must share with one another, even to laying down one's life for the other. Then the Pope gave some sage advice and I will never forget that either. It was so strange to see such an important person give everyday advice to the several thousand people assembled from all walks of life.

'Whenever you ring someone on the telephone,' His Holiness said, 'always ask, "Are you free to speak to me?" Don't just start talking without checking that it is convenient to the person you are calling. This is good manners.' I was amazed that Pope Shenouda III should be concerned with something so ordinary as telephone manners. I was witnessing a father instructing his children – that simple! More surprises were to come.

One after another, his secretary opened small sheets of paper and read out questions people had written to the Pope. This great man, directly in line of office with St Mark, the writer of the Gospel, spoke to his people, several thousand silent souls taking in every word. Some of the questions regarded doctrine about divorce or fasting or family matters, about immigration and the forcing of Christian children to learn the Koran. When he finished, the cathedral erupted into wild applause, with women ululating, filling the cathedral with shrills of joy.

Then the Pope proceeded down the central aisle, blessing his people, followed by the bonneted desert monks and the parish priests.

****

> I will praise you, O Lord,
> among the nations;
> I will sing of you among the peoples.
> For great is your love,
> reaching to the heavens;
> your faithfulness reaches to the skies.
> Be exalted, O God, above the heavens;
> let your glory be over all the earth.

Psalm 57 v 9 – 11

Chapter Forty Four

Holy Mountain

The diamond necklace of hundreds of torches wove in and out, winding slowly, slowly upwards. Against the jewelled sky, thick with the northern constellations, the black outline of the great mountain loomed.

The slow loping movement of Ahmed and the gentle clicking of Saleem, his Bedouin owner, added to the almost overwhelming feeling of 'over-ness'. I asked Saleem if Ahmed knew the way in the dark.

He answered with what I suspected was a well-used phrase: 'Ahmed values his life more than yours'.

****

I remember the time I negotiated my first night journey upon the Mountain of God, Mount Horeb. I had recently had knee surgery and six weeks later I was climbing Mt Sinai with a much younger woman called Sandy McPherson. She was an ex-physical educationist and still very fit, with long legs made to stride one step to my two. Making matters even more challenging for me, another younger woman joined us.

'Hi, my name is Alicia. Could I join you two gals for the night and the trip up?'

We were the only unaccompanied women on the bus through the Sinai, so it was appropriate for her to be with us. Sandy and I had intended to mark our historic journey by reading the ancient text of the book of Exodus. We were concerned that our new companion might interfere with this. Alicia, a New York lawyer on an 'after a failed love affair' trip around the world, had other designs for her Mt Sinai visit.

'I've just climbed Mt Kilimanjaro. A four day trek, then the climb.'

We nodded knowingly and Sandy laughed and chatted about desert crossings and when was the best time to visit Petra.

'Next stop's the Athens' marathon,' Alicia said. 'It'll be the seventh I've run this year. Would you wake me at three am? Thanks.'

Alicia said this while stretching her gorgeous long tanned limbs from her tiny khaki shorts. She ran her hands through the ropes of blond tresses cascading down her back. She bunched a hank of it on top of her head. Then she secured it with an elaborate wooden African carved pin. She lay back on her bed and promptly went to sleep. My heart sank almost to the level of my mending meniscus.

'How on earth will I keep up with her?'

'Oh, we'll let her go at her own pace. We won't let her spoil our plans.'

Good old Sandy with the long, long legs and the aerobic capacity of a long distance runner. And sure enough, once we started out with the stars like electric lights hung from a trellis, Alicia and Sandy both disappeared from sight.

I puffed my way up to each bend of the leg of thin white track exposed by a tiny sliver of moon. At each turning upwards the two of them would wait. The moment I joined them they would promptly take off. I'd double over, gasping great gulps of thinning air into my lungs.

Then I'd hear the first of the quiet calls from the shadows: 'Camel, miss? Only fifty pounds'.

At four am I found Sandy talking with an elderly couple, part of a contingent of pilgrims from the Philippines. They were having trouble breathing, too, and were surprisingly carrying no water. I gave them my bottle of Baraka filled with spring water from the Siwa Oasis.

As we moved on, Sandy explained that she had let Alicia go ahead.

Night Journeys

At dawn we passed her coming down at a neat trot, calling out: 'I've met this cute Dutch boy and he'll share his taxi with me to the Israeli border. Thanks for the share of your room. Bye.'

Our New York lawyer hadn't even waited for the sun to strike the summit before she bounded off the mountain and out of our lives forever.

Many of the pilgrims had taken camels to the thousand steps. Then it was every pilgrim for themselves. Only donkeys ventured further. Shy, black-veiled, colourful-skirted Bedouin girls guided them. Their packs carried chocolate and soft drinks for the little food stalls dotting the summit. These stalls offered carpeted space for weary bodies to lie, to sit, and perchance to sip sweet cardamom coffee. Egyptian-made Cadbury's chocolates, gritty and tasteless, were sold for exorbitant prices.

Each step up the thousand steps was a personal triumph. The surrounding landscape transformed: first gold, orange, deep rust, and then shades of vermilion as the early rays of the morning sun struck each rock. In the distance, the rolling hills disappeared into misty mauve. I thought of the Australian outback, particularly the Olgas, so familiar were the colours.

As the sun crept higher, hundreds of pilgrims who had made the major climb by camel were coming down from the summit. One woman clad in colourful shawls called out, her arms wide open:

'Columbia. I'm from Columbia.' She reached me.

Our eyes locked.

With my arms wide open, I called to her, 'Australia. I'm from Australia.'

We hugged each other.

Upon this sacred spot where the nations gathered to walk in the footsteps of Moses, we embraced.

Then she was gone.

Sandy and I continued our climb. We took two and a half hours to reach the summit. Then Sandy had an attack of hypothermia. There I was, the unfit one, funnelling ghastly powdered Egyptian milk chocolate down her throat. Then the strengthening sun began resurrecting the cold bodies on the mountaintop.

The old Filipino couple had made it. Still clasping my *baraka* bottle, they asked us to join their group for Holy Communion. We were thrilled.

We watched as a tall man pulled out of his backpack lovely embroidered vestments, a stole, and a wooden box with the Holy Eucharist within. We were not Catholics, but this group of worshipping people wanted to include us. We shared this holy time together and found ourselves being hugged by twenty strangers who were no longer strangers.

Night Journeys

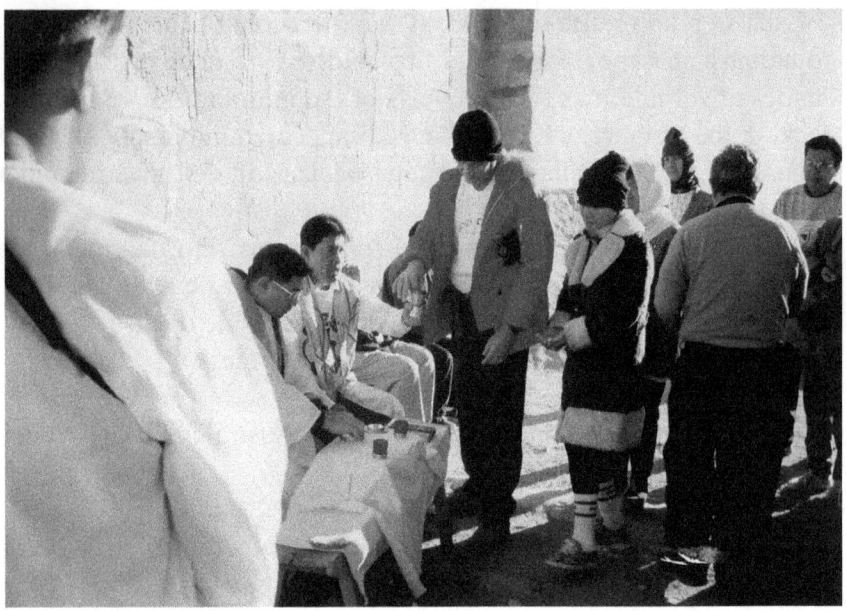

Soon the mountain shed its human cargo. We spent four hours enjoying the clean air, the rare beauty, the absolute quiet, and the sheer holiness of the place. We read our Bibles, reliving the Exodus experience. We came across a group of Hasidic Israeli boys in full regalia with long side curls and fringed shawls.

'How'd you think two million people could fit down there?' one boy asked, indicating the endless hills rolling out from the mountain.

We speculated about positioning, and using the scriptures, we agreed on the most important thing, that in Exodus 19:20 it said, 'The LORD descended to the top of Mount Sinai.' And here we were!

Later, the sun rose higher in the brilliant sky where no smog ever visited. Sandy and I worked our way down the longer route. It was so steep you couldn't see two steps before you. As our feet touched a rock, the next step appeared.

It was truly a faith walk.

Raylene Pearce

The way we had chosen was called the Pilgrim's Way.
It was dotted with ancient hermit caves, stone cottages, and amazingly beautiful archways of un-mortared stone built centuries ago.

****

I thought of the women I met or heard about on my night journeys. Of the nameless ones working the Thai brothels of Hat Jai and the little lady whom I ignored, with bells on her shoulders, begging in the street, and the rescued one Basanti and her mother Asha, in Nepal.
Of the women taking on small businesses and writing their stories in rural Nepal and India, and of Rami and her 'sisters' in the Ladies'

Night Journeys

Waiting Room on Gorakhpur Station, India. Of Felicity travelling her dark journey towards the light.

I thought with thanks of my close Egyptian friend, Nevine, who had never spent a night out of her family circle, but came on Retreat with me. I thought of my Christian Egyptian women colleagues, so talented and able to produce television programmes and create magazines.

I thought of the Egyptian women I interviewed who were independent, smart of mind, and beautiful of face.

I thought of my Western colleagues who left the security of home to go to the far country on the leading of God; many of them, because of the isolation of their posting, missing out on meeting a husband and having children of their own.

I thought of Ananeke who let me stay with her trip after trip to Egypt, who had such a gentle heart for Egyptian children with disabilities and their families.

I thought of Jillian and meeting her in the skies above Turkey with her writing a postcard to me. I remembered Kirsty McDonald, and sitting with her beside her peat fire on an island at the end of the earth, praying to Jesus.

I thought of the Columbian woman who embraced me on the holy mountain and the elderly Filipino lady who asked us to share the Holy Communion, and the shy Bedouin girl with her donkey.

I thought of Alicia who couldn't wait for sunrise and Sandy shading her hand over her eyes, gazing down at the monastery before our final descent of Mt Sinai.

All strong women—some of us free and some not so free, with others little more than slaves.

All worth remembering and celebrating!

****

Then down at the monastery Sandy and I ate bread, cheese, and olives, washed down with St Catherine's red wine while sitting beside Jethro's well.

I thought of his daughter Zipporah, Moses's wife, who went with him to Pharaoh demanding that he let their people go.

She was strong too.

****

Now the LORD had said to Moses in Midian,
"Go back to Egypt,
for all the men who wanted to kill you are dead."
So Moses took his wife and sons, put them on a donkey
and started back to Egypt.
And he took the staff of God in his hand.

Exodus 4 v 19 & 20

****

Chapter Forty Five

Everything Changes

Mediterranean MEMoirs   August 2001.   No 4:2

It was the thirty-sixth flat I'd seen! I had looked and looked and nothing was right...too expensive, too dreadful, or too inappropriate for a single woman to live in etc. etc.

One Saturday after walking the streets looking for two flats ....one address was the wrong number in the right street and the other was the wrong street and the right number! I came home exhausted, asking God what all this wasted time and energy was about.

Returning to this place from Home Assignment in Adelaide had been marred by the need to look for another dwelling because my landlord had raised the rent.

That night my landlord's sister came to me and asked for the rent. I said I couldn't pay at the rates they were now demanding and that I was looking for another flat.

The following day she told me that her brother, who was still out of the country, had lowered the rent to the previous rate and I agreed to stay. I had no lease and I continued to live in a five-floor building as the only tenant!

But now, my landlord and his sisters have decided to leave the country altogether! This means I need to find a new flat as soon as possible. This could prove to be a stressful experience so your prayers would be appreciated.

Raylene Pearce

Dec 30th 2014
I've just found this article in a pile of letters I've been going through. As I read the final paragraph I realised that I had forgotten about my landlord's plans to return to Germany for good sometime in July/August 2001. Another puzzle!

****

Everything continues to change.

At the end of the school year in June of 2001 our international community dispersed, leaving me very lonely in our building.

Sadly, I said goodbye to Felicity, Mark, and Holly. After three very productive years of working in media with our media company they felt called to return to Liverpool and I grieved that they were no longer in Egypt.

As the apartments emptied, Sabry asked me to look about for replacement tenants. During the summer months it was always hard to find new people. The huge city would empty of millions of people who were able to leave. Rich expatriates or well-off Egyptians would head off to the Red Sea, the Gulf of Aqaba, or the North African coastline. This exodus reminded me of my holiday at Mersa Matruah with my kind Egyptian friends four years before. It wasn't always the rich people going to the coast but Coptic Christians and Evangelical Christians saving up to holiday together.

In August the city began to fill with newcomers for the beginning of the school year, so I brought up the subject of tenants again.

This time Sabry seemed distracted and not interested.

'I don't know what I want to do. I'll let you know.'

****

He had let the vacant flats deteriorate, allowing sand to leach through splintered window frames and gaping holes where air conditioners had once been.

I remember one occasion when Sabry gave me a key to show some people from Australia through one of the apartments. They were unimpressed because of the neglect. Sabry made no attempt to prepare the flats for occupancy.

One afternoon I heard a palaver outside my first floor living room window. I watched, unseen, as Sabry and his sisters clambered down from the front seat of a huge tow truck. Their damaged car was then parked beside the ficus trees.

Later I met Sabry on the stairs. His face was pale and he stared at me. He was very shocked and complained of a headache. He said that they had been run off the Desert Road on their way back from Alexandria.

'A car picked us out and deliberately ran us off the road.' He looked weird and then said, 'I think it was the CIA.'

'Why would the CIA be interested in you?' was my inane reply, but Sabry brushed my query off and hurried up the stairs.

I tended to do that. Whenever anyone told me something awful or strange like the CIA running you off the road, I'd cover my shock by asking an oblique question, never something straight like, 'How did you know it was the CIA?'

The next day Sabry came to my door. 'You have to look for another apartment.'

'You mean now? You want me to go now? I thought you wanted more tenants?'

'I've changed my mind. I'm sorry, you must start looking now.'

This was a hard ask. Available, affordable flats were becoming rare as new expatriates filled the city and prices were rising by the week. I was still on a tight budget. I told Sabry I would start to look but it would take some time.

The next day he flew to Germany and I was given a reprieve. I neither heard nor saw the girls but I knew they were in the building. When I came back from work in the evenings, a tiny light peeped from the upstairs flat and sometimes a noise floated down to the first floor.

I tried not to get spooked living in a skeleton of a five story building with two elusive young women on the 4th and 5th floor. Sand blasted down the open stairwell. Most of the buildings of our type have the top window of the stairwell open – no glass – just open to the elements. It rarely rained but the sand and dust were pervasive and Sabry changed policy and refused to allow anyone to come onto the property to clean or maintain the place.

The idea of moving was becoming a much more attractive option.

One afternoon I was visiting my colleagues to practice an item for the church fete. Our church was 1,000 strong with forty plus nationalities. The Annual Fete was a celebration of the different cultures, all Christians worshipping together. While people were eating the assorted foods of the nations, different groups sang or danced, children and adults together.

With some other Aussies we were practising two numbers, *'The Great Southland of the Holy Spirit'* and *'Waltzing Matilda'*.

I made a call. 'Liz aren't you going to join us?'

'A plane's just flown into the World Trade Centre in New York!'

'What sort of plane?' I was thinking of a small aircraft clipping a corner.

'I don't know. CBS is covering it.'

One of my favourite memories of New York was when I stood on the top of the World Trade Centre in December 1999, the Empire State Building in the distance, with my friend Rosemary Boehm who was the US Representative of our Media Company.

Now the whole building was apparently collapsing in flames!

Night Journeys

From 4.30 pm Cairo time I stayed glued to my friends' television with other shocked Australians until 11 pm when I finally gathered the courage to make my way home.

Everything's changed now, I thought. What will the world be like?

I had a nightmare walk along a dark tunnel-like street, the trees touching overhead. I had walked this way many times before but I didn't feel safe any more. The street ran into the madness of the *Midan el Ittihad*. Five lanes of traffic curled their snakelike way around the defunct fountain.

There were dozens of trucks, horns blasting, going in circles around the *midan*, laden with young Egyptian men, fists in the air, shouting and cheering as though *Ahly* had won the soccer final!

It was surreal. I was a lone, foreign woman, standing on the edge of the pit of hell, as pent-up hatred for the West spewed out like thick black exhaust fumes from every vehicle and foul breath from every open mouth.

****

After what seemed an age, relief flooded me when a taxi finally stopped and I crawled into the relative safety of the little black and white car.

'Now Amreeka knows what it's like to be bombed,' my gloating taxi driver sneered as he wound his way through the packed streets to the front gate of No. 352.

I didn't ask him what he meant. I knew he wouldn't have personally been bombed lately. But everything in this area of the world comes down to one thing – Palestine. That's what he's talking about. The hatred of American foreign policy is prolific. It's a bizarre mindset. Ask anyone where they would like to live and they'll all say, "Amreeka".

Early the next morning I heard Sabry and his sisters clanking their way through the front gate laden with enough bags of vegetables and groceries to withstand a prolonged siege.

Sabry knocked on my door and sharply said:

'You have to leave. Now!'

'What, now? I leave just like that?'

'All right, I want you out by the end of the week.' Sabry looked so peculiar, no longer the suave educated young landlord who had urged me to live in his apartment house one year before. His eyes were screwed up and he looked white around the mouth. I thought of my friends who had lived in this building with Sabry as their pleasant landlord – they would not have recognised him now!

'How's your headache, Sabry?'

'It's nothing. Concussion, that's all.'

'If you're concussed you must see a doctor.'

'No time for that. You leave by the end of the week.'

Even though expatriates had been told to stay off the streets, I went for a walk around the block, asking the *bowabs,* the doorkeepers, if there were any vacant flats.

The Nubian man who swept my street came up to me and said, pointing a long bony finger at my chest:

'*Inti Ortstraylia? Aiwah?*'

I wanted to say, '*La'a. Ana Amrikana*' to see the look on his face, but I was too stressed to play games. The tension on the street was tangible, making me imagine that I was under more scrutiny than usual. I could feel suspicious eyes following me. I could no longer hide among my once friendly neighbours. My own home no longer offered me security. I was unwanted. Even so, I felt that with the current crisis and an inner assurance that my work here was far from over, I needed to find a flat nearby where I wasn't a complete stranger.

Within a week I had signed a lease on a flat just around the corner. What provision!

Night Journeys

On the day I left No. 352, Sabry, still manifesting the headache he'd had since the Desert Road crash, saw me to the gate.

'Sabry, you must go to the doctor!' My voice rising in desperation, I went on to say, 'I think you're concussed; quite possibly bleeding into your brain. I can find you a doctor. Let me help you.'

He slowly shook his head. The Sabry I once thought I knew had disappeared.

I went back that night and tried to see Sabry but he wouldn't talk to me. The sisters refused to let me in.

I screamed through the intercom at the gate, 'I have the phone number of a local neurosurgeon. You must take this phone number, or your brother will die!'

'Leave it in the letter box,' one of the girls yelled back.

And I did.

And that was the last I saw of them.

What on earth was going on?

****

STOP THE PRESS

Mediterranean MEMoirs to my supporters: 11/11/2001

I watched in horror as the events unfolded in the United States, like so many of you did. I happened to ring a colleague who was watching CNN just as the second plane flew into the south tower of the World Trade Centre. I was at a meeting at the time and we had access to CNN and stayed glued in shock for hours.

Later that night it was very uncomfortable walking through the dark streets until I found a taxi to take me home. There I phoned around to all my American friends who were still here – most had gone home for the summer. Once again watching TV as our friends in America were suffering was an incomprehensible and truly horrible experience.

Many of you have prayed for me over the years with the many travelling experiences I have had. I took more than 200 flights in the last 7 years, without real incident. I always trusted the security systems at airports and this was in many different countries: Cyprus, Egypt, Jordan, Israel, Lebanon, Greece, Turkey, five times to the USA, Canada, Holland, Germany, countless times to the UK, Malaysia, Indonesia, Thailand, Singapore, Nepal, India, and I landed once in Sri Lanka!

I make a habit as I settle into my seat of committing all the passengers on board to the Lord and the pilots and staff. I finish with '*Underneath are the everlasting arms.*' I imagine God holding us up and I fold into the seat confident of his care.

Events are still unfolding and because of certain connections being made I covet your prayers that the response to this shocking act, will be God driven. We have been told to keep a low profile, but it's really been a very quiet and ordinary day here in this huge city.

I pray for you all too, as you think through all this. Please do not place wickedness onto a whole people group. This has been planned and carried out by wicked people, marginal people, when the majority of people in this part of the world hate what has happened and grieve along with you.

I have to trust in God for everything, and so do you. I cannot understand what has happened but I know our God can bring good out of the evil men do. My thoughts are out to all those people who are still waiting for the news of missing relations and friends and those whose grief is immense through the confirmed loss of loved ones.

Night Journeys

The aftermath of the attack on the United States of America and the free world community was that our various NGO's met and put into effect the contingency plans that would apply if conditions in this country deteriorated.

As time went on the situation did deteriorate in Egypt. It was discovered that some Egyptians were complicit in the attacks. It was suggested that we single women move in together or with a family. We'd close ranks. We would each have a case packed with our valuables – passport, laptops, and US dollars always close at hand. But no one wanted to leave.

Other companies were sending their American volunteers home. Our policy was that, as long as we weren't a danger to any of our local staff, we stay put. It was sad when we were told not to visit our Egyptian friends because of the verbal abuse they were getting from their usually friendly neighbours. It was all back to front; wasn't this an attack on the West? Why were they making us feel guilty?

****

May the God of peace,
who through the blood of the eternal covenant
brought back from the dead our Lord Jesus,
the Shepherd of the sheep,
equip you with everything good for doing his will,
and may he work in us what is pleasing to him,
through Jesus Christ,
to whom be glory for ever and ever. Amen.

James 13 v 20 & 21

Chapter Forty Six

New world, new flat, new friends

A grey-haired gentleman; his moustache neatly shaped under the brown skin of his fine Egyptian nose; his shoulders pushed back into his grey suit; his fine white shirt and deep blue tie tight against his chest; his walking stick with a mother-of-pearl handle leaning on the arm of the chair; his deep set eyes looking at me. He gave me a shock when I first saw him. He looked like a person posing in a sepia photo, so formal and straight did he sit.

'Why do you want to live in this apartment?' he asked.

'It's very nice; it's near to where I used to live; I have friends nearby; and it's in my price range.'

He spoke the amount he was asking for the rent. Way over what I thought I needed to pay! The agent had assured me that this first floor flat, just around the corner from my old place, was in my price range.

'I'm sorry. My allowance does not let me to pay this amount. I can only afford 750 pounds.' I sighed and stood up. Then as I turned towards the door I stopped, turned to him and said, 'Mr Ghali, there will not be any foreigners coming to live in this city for a very long time. I would have been an excellent tenant, but I have a restriction on how much I can pay.'

I took a step towards the door when he spoke. 'You can have it for 800 pounds.'

Mousa, his son, who would be the one collecting the rent, stood and brought out the papers to sign. Smiles all round.

Mr Ghali stood and said, 'Mrs Ghali and I would like you to come to our home for a meal. Mousa will give you the details.'

And with a nod of his elegant head he shook my hand and said goodbye.

Night Journeys

Mr and Mrs Ghali were both retired lawyers. Mrs Ghali was one of the first females to be allowed to study in the university and among the first women graduates of Cairo University with a law degree. They had a daughter who disappeared some years before to join her husband in Afghanistan and had never been heard of since. Mousa and his wife were childless so the immediate family was small and carried their sorrow with dignity.

Over the next four years when I was their 'excellent' tenant, Mousa and I became friends. We would discuss many issues over a cup of tea when he came for the rent. I ate with his parents on several occasions. I always brought flowers from the ubiquitous flower stalls, as I knew that Mrs Ghali always appreciated them.

My friends and colleagues helped me move. It wasn't until I settled in that I noticed the minaret outlined between the two buildings in front of mine.

A five times a day reminder to pray. And five times a day I tried to block out the prayers. The prayers were amplified from the mosque. On Friday, the set sermon screamed its angry message across the suburbs.

I was the only non-Muslim in the apartment block and the only single foreign female in the vicinity. I became a source of interest from the first day, as the United States and allies began bombing suspected al Qaeda and Taliban positions in Afghanistan.

****

What is it about me, and keys and locks? It's my first day in the new flat. My hand is poised, the key goes into the lock. Nothing. I try it again. Nothing. I turn it upside down. That's worked before on other recalcitrant locks. Not this time. I look at the door. Look at the key. I can't work it out. When we moved the stuff in the door was open. Was I given the wrong key?

While I was pondering these questions the door opposite opened and a man came out.

'The lock is a problem? Let me try.'

Taking the key from me, he proceeded to have as much luck as I.

Before I could make any suggestions regarding contacting my landlord, he sent out a little boy into the street to find a locksmith. The landing was now filled with people: several children and a woman wearing a shapeless long floral gown to the floor and a wrap-around scarf. Below the scarf was a friendly smile.

'I am Mahmoud and this is my wife Hanan,' he said indicating the lady with the friendly smile. 'These are my children. You must come into our home and wait for the locksmith.'

And I did just that. This was my introduction to neighbourly Egyptian hospitality. I was seated on an ornate chair and immediately presented with mango juice you could stand a spoon up in. While I sipped this wonderful elixir, Hanan stood in front of me and chatted non-

Night Journeys

stop in Arabic. From time to time I would nod and say *'aiwah,'* which means yes. This was enough to encourage her more. The children sat or stood around their mother, watching their guest. I felt like a specimen under the microscope but was inwardly thrilled that I had such friendly neighbours.

As I gazed at the hundred names of Allah, within a gold picture frame, Fatima, the oldest girl, came in with some cakes. Fatima was sixteen years old and, even though she was in her own home, had her hair covered. I was supposed to eat the cream cakes while everyone watched. No one joined me. Even my offering a piece of cake to little Lila produced more streams of Arabic, but no intention of eating or drinking with me. Abdul Rackman was twelve and Ali was ten. Renee was fourteen and she seemed to be in charge of the little two-year-old Lila, who looked longingly at the cake but was not given permission to join me.

Once the locksmith arrived, Mahmoud insisted on overseeing the opening of my door. Thus began an interesting relationship with my over-the-passageway neighbours. They seemed to know whenever I arrived in my flat. No sooner had I shut my door, there would be a little knock. Standing in front of me, one of the children would appear holding a plate of some wonderful food that Hanan had cooked.

Only once could I not eat what was offered me. I was presented with dirty brown lumpy spongy pieces of something in a bowl. I asked what it was and I was told it was lung! Imagine eating the lungs of cows breathing the smog of Cairo – or any other air for that matter. I took my gift to language class and the students all gagged and the teachers chewed, delight flooding their faces! No accounting for taste – as someone once said.

Hanan never left the building without her husband, or her sons. The girls could only leave the building in the company of their younger brothers. Only the boys went to the mosque with their father. Hanan moved about the apartment house freely, visiting the Iman upstairs with the girls in tow, or chatting on the landings with other residents. They were a loving family and gradually over the four years I lived near them I got to know their story.

Mahmoud saw Hanan on the bus. They worked at the same engineering works and he had glimpsed her face as she boarded the bus and he fell in love with her smile. He asked about her and was introduced to her cousin who also worked in the factory.

Through that introduction, he and his parents were invited to have afternoon tea with Hanan's family. During this time it was ascertained that they were of similar education and financial status. Various enquiries were made about their reputations and piety. They were officially engaged on the second visit and this enabled them to spend some time together. With a member of the family always present, Mahmoud and Hanan chatted over endless cups of tea.

When Mahmoud and Hanan married they went to live in one of the satellite cities in the desert. Egyptians hate living away from their inner families. This was an ordeal for the pregnant Hanan. Not having a mother and sisters around during this time, she was very lonely. She loved her husband but they both missed their families.

The two sisters were born while they lived in Sadat City. I've been there. It's modern with tree-lined streets, but if you visit on a weekend it's deserted. The inhabitants return to their beloved Cairo. They miss the noise, the people, the buzz, and mother's cooking.

****

What Price Friendship?

I walk out of my apartment. There's Mahmoud, bending over the boot of his car.

He stands up, sees me and says, 'I see a vision. Is this really you? Where have you been? Why haven't we seen you?'

I put on a droopy face. 'I've been sick.'

'Why didn't you let us know? We could have come and looked after you.'

'Oh, I prefer staying in bed under the quilt and not having anyone around.'

'No, that is not right. Hanan would have cared for you, cooked for you, made you well.'

'Thank you so much, but my friends sent me food. I just wanted to be left alone.'

'What?' snaps Mahmoud, 'You stopped us getting merit from God because you didn't let us look after you!'

That silences me for an instant.

Then I say, 'You mean, because you are such kind people, you want to care for me?'

'No.' says Mahmoud. 'When we look after you we receive merit from God'.

To make sure I have this right, I ask, 'Is it because you and Hanan are kind that you want to care for me?'

'No! We must earn merit with God for our good deeds. You have prevented us from earning merit, especially Hanan!'

'Isn't it because you like me?'

'No, you don't understand. We could have earned real merit if you had allowed us to look after you when you were sick.'

I say, 'But you don't have to earn merit with God'.

Mahmoud says, 'Yes we do.'

'No, you don't.'

'Yes, we do.'

'No, you don't.'

It's starting to sound like a number from *Annie Get Your Gun*.

I don't remember learning this technique at Bible College. My Principal said once, 'Raylene, you are the most illogical student I have ever had,' then a pause, 'but the most entertaining.'

Mahmoud and I part amicably, with me promising to catch up with them all later. He's worried about Hanan because women have to have loads of merit to be even considered for occupancy in paradise. There is no mention in the Koran of women going to heaven. Only the ever-lasting virgins given to martyrs get a place in the hereafter.

There's no assurance for anyone. If your good deeds don't outweigh your bad deeds at your death, you're doomed. No one knows if they have enough merit—a terrible way to live your life and to die your death.

****

I feel deflated.
I thought they liked me.
Now I know that all I am to them is a 'merit provider'.

What a downer!

****

I was asked to write the Christmas Play for the Maadi Community Church. I called it 'To the Ends of the Earth' and told the story from the Creation of the world, the Incarnation of the birth of Jesus, his ministry, death, and resurrection, culminating in the movement of the Christian faith throughout the world.

Our church had over forty nationalities so we were able to acknowledge the Gospel coming to many of our countries. A woman from Ireland acknowledged the Egyptian missionaries who are buried in her country. They brought the Good News to her people in the first centuries after the death and resurrection of Jesus Christ.

We had a Brazilian Mary and a Nigerian Joseph. One wise man was from Sudan, one from England and another from America. Jesus was a Filipino baby, called Jesus (how about that?) and Gabriel was a glorious young woman whose mother was Lebanese and father from the United States. Elizabeth was from England married to an Egyptian and her husband Zachariah was played by Norm Tucker from South Australia. Our Narrator was Afro-American.

To top it all off, St Mark, the writer of the Gospel and the first patriarch of the Egyptian church, came on stage. A lovely Egyptian Christian man played the part and we felt completed. Here we were in this amazing country, many of us brought to Egypt by the call of God on our lives to partner the church in Egypt and to share Christ with the people of the Middle East. Now, we were together acknowledging the place of Egypt in the spread of the gospel.

****

A great joy for me was that Mahmoud, Hanan, and the children came to the play. They stayed around at the end and met Gabriel and spoke with our Canadian minister David Pretescue.

****

Raylene Pearce

In that day there will be an altar to the LORD
in the heart of Egypt,
and a monument to the LORD at its border.
It will be a sign and witness to the LORD Almighty
in the land of Egypt.

When they call out to the LORD
because of their oppressors,
he will send them a saviour and defender,
and he will rescue them.

So the LORD will make himself known
to the Egyptians,
and in that day they will acknowledge the LORD.

The prophecy of Isaiah 19 v 19 – 21, 23 – 25

The Monastery of Al Muharraq, at the geographical heart of Egypt where Isaiah's prophecy is fulfilled, as the Holy Communion is celebrated every day.

Chapter Forty Seven

Raining in Egypt

I'm being told how to get rid of my cold. I'm told that lemon and honey and lots of *shay* (tea) will do the trick. I listen and nod, and cough my head off while billows of smoke pour over me from my friendly taxi driver's cigarette.

The sandstorm hit on the first day of the Iraq war. I'm at home taking my second course of antibiotics. I make a quick sortie into the street, around the corner, to the local *souk* to get some needed provisions.

I chat with the greengrocer. 'Yes it's a great shame. We had been praying that a war would not start. We now pray that it will be short.'

I want to touch base with my friends here. I don't want to hide from my Egyptian neighbours just because the Prime Minister of Australia was on TV last night. Even before Tony Blair gets permission from his government, John Howard is grinning into the camera and declaring, for all the world to hear, that his troops will be fighting with the 'Coalition of the Willing'. He's declaring he's a mate of George Bush! The most hated man in the Middle East. So where does that leave me? I'm the only Australian living within my section of Maadi where about one million people live in high-rise buildings.

I make my way home laden with my purchases braced against the wind, my scarf wrapped around my mouth. After the sandstorm, the rain comes, gentle and persistent, and makes all the locals panic. People ring family throughout the city, checking the state of roads, checking walls, checking water seeping through cracks from flat roofs.

Mud takes over. There are no drains in the city of Cairo. It only rains two or three days a year; no need for storm water drains. Today is a fluke.

Raylene Pearce

Later that day I have to get keys cut for guests. I'd rather be hiding from my neighbours under the quilt and not becoming a merit provider, but because I am ill, I will not be picking my visitors up from the airport in the middle of the night. So I need to take keys to the friends who will do it for me. Driving through the sprinkling rain, the afternoon light yellow and eerie, my taxi driver peers through his windscreen and says, 'How can they fight a war in this?'

I get another set of keys cut and leave the old ones with my friends to give to my guests so they can let themselves into my apartment block with one key, and with the second key into my flat. I return home with the new ones. This taxi's windscreen wipers are covered in mud—it's raining mud. Through the blurred landscape we arrive home in one piece.

The new key allows me access through the front door into the foyer but no one (not even Mohammed, my doorman) can turn the second key in my flat door! My blood sugar's low and my nerves on edge, my nose is running and I don't want to be seen by Mahmoud. It's getting colder and the sky darker. Too tired and hungry to go back to the locksmith I return to my friend's house and retrieve my old key to my flat. So my guests have the outside key to at least get off the street but I will now have to wait up for them to let them into my flat.

I proceed home.

The rain has washed away the smog – no more mud - and now pelts down in swathes. This time, my taxi doesn't even have windscreen wipers! We both peer through the water-veined glass. The driver has his nose to the windscreen, trying to discern what is going on in front of him. He doesn't have his lights on, which would have helped. The locals are convinced that leaving your lights on while driving runs down the battery. It can also blind the eyes of people walking on the road (true), and, most importantly, direct Israeli gunfire when the next war against them starts!

I continue to give directions to my driver, calling into his ear in Arabic and applauding his amazing driving skills. As we draw outside my building we look at each other and laugh. Rain drives people mad here.

Night Journeys

My guests from the UK arrive early the next morning with my outside key in hand. I'm waiting to let them in, cradling a hot water bottle.

Evelyn says, 'It's colder here than in London.'

I'm dressed in a woollen skirt, jumper, and long cardigan with my long Bristol-blue full-length coat and lace-up boots. I look at Eve. She is in a light-blue blouse, a light-cream summer-weight jacket, and short skirt with gorgeous legs and ankles for the locals to gawk at.

We'll deal with that tomorrow.

I produce one of my warmer scarves.

Should I wrap it around her neck or her legs?

The Iraq war is twenty-four hours old and it's still raining in Egypt.

****

Trust in the LORD and do good;
dwell in the land and enjoy safe pasture.
Delight yourself in the LORD and he will give you
the desires of your heart...

Commit your way to the LORD,
Trust also in him,
and he shall bring it to pass.
He shall bring forth your righteousness as the light,
and your justice as the noonday.

Psalm 37 v 5, 6

Raylene Pearce

Run Raylene Run!

I had been visiting an asthmatic child. The mother and I had sat for some hours watching her and waiting to see if we needed to take her to hospital. As the dawn neared we decided she was well enough for me to leave, so I set off for my flat, two blocks away. It was about 4am.

As I rounded the corner, from out of an empty block on my right, a pack of wild, yellow, barking, probably rabid dogs set upon me. I stepped towards them. I gave a huge shout – 'GOoooooo' and clapped my hands. I took another step towards them, clapping my hands and yelling.

They cowered.

Then, as I turned and walked swiftly down the street they gathered themselves and started after me again. It was frightful. We did this macarbe dance, back and forth, back and forth. The yelling and the clapping, the howling and the barking, the turning and returning; the gradual moving dance-step by dance-step towards home.

I came in sight of my apartment house. On the far corner of my street just past my home the night guard leaned on his AK47. I gave another outburst to the dogs. I ran in the middle of the street towards the soldier and my front door but my possible rescuer just kept puffing on his cigarette. I don't think he got what was happening.

I was about to be eaten by rabid dogs!

This time my key worked.

****

Night Journeys

Night Time Drama

I can't believe myself!

For nights on end they have been digging up the footpath and guttering outside my flat in the middle of the night and keeping me awake.

So here I am out on the balcony in my nightie, yelling at the security guys. They are making huge cracking noises that ricochet off the surrounding buildings right into my bedroom!

It's 3.30am!

It's not till the next morning that James (my son who is staying with me while he works with Sudanese refugees) tells me that they were only breaking wood to put on their little fires to keep warm!

Next time I prance around on my balcony in the middle of the night, I must wear my glasses!

****

My Balcony

Let me take you out on my *balakona*, as they say in Egyptian Arabic. I'm balancing on a stool, balancing my laptop on my lap.

Below on the street corner of the busy intersection three guards stand, dressed in their summer whites, AK47's slung over their shoulders. They lounge about, watching everything and hopefully doing something if needed. The other night when I was chased by seven dogs, they just stood and watched! But they did help when I couldn't open my door one night (habit of mine) and we always exchange greetings each time I cross the street.

Right now a blue ribbon is floating by with a wee basket attached. The children above me are lowering it for some reason.

Here is an endless stream of traffic; there's a bus filled to the brim; three cars pass below; now a man on a bicycle with beams of wood balancing on his left shoulder; two guys standing in the middle of the intersection talking; now some taxis; they are everywhere and my main form of cheap transport.

There's a man with no legs. He rolls around on a plank with wheels like a giant skateboard while at work in the bicycle shop on the corner. When he goes home each night he drives an elaborate hand operated bicycle.

The little basket has just gone by with lemons in it!

People stroll along the street, easier to walk on, as the footpaths tend to disappear. The mosque in the next street, open to view between the buildings opposite, is silent for a while. It has a flame tree growing at its base.

I've just put some sweets into the wee basket; that should give them a treat, much more interesting than lemons!

One of the times we had our water cut off, two girls walked under my *balakona* with huge tin dishes on their heads filled with water. The hairdresser next door has afforded me much entertainment when the white clad, tulle stiffened brides leave, to attend their receptions. Their hordes of female relatives pore out of the shop, pack into dozens of cars, and honk their way through the streets. *Honk. Honk. Honk-honk-honk.* They block the roads. One night I counted eight buses stuck from four streets unable to enter the intersection because of the latest bridal procession from the hairdresser.

Everyone honks then.

It's after 6pm, sun still high, still warm.

The girls' mother has just come to the door to greet me after my little gift of sweets. My Arabic is still poor but I get away with it because the people know I care about them. Come to think about it, what did she come for?

Clang, clang, clang. A man is banging the sides of a gas cylinder on his bike. He wants the servants or the daughters to bring down the empty gas cylinders so he can go and fill them.

The basket has just lowered; there's a note. I read it. It's in English. 'Great it's nice fun. Thank you very much but we are not four!! We are five plus one (servant) Gamal's family.'

I find more sweets and send them up. So there you go. You never know what you are in for when you visit my *balakona*.

My door bell full of twittering birds has gone berserk again. There stands a little girl about 10 years old (the servant of the sixth sweet).

She says '*Shokrun, inti gamela awy.*'
'Thank you, you are beautiful, very.'

****

'I tell you the truth,' Jesus replied,
'No one who has left home or brothers or sisters or mother
or father or children or fields for me and the gospel
will fail to receive a hundred times as much in this present age
(homes, brothers, sisters, mothers, children, and fields -
and with them persecutions)
and in the age to come, eternal life.

Mark 10 V 29 & 30

Chapter Forty Eight

Back to the Future

In January 2003 Jan Fielke came to Egypt to work in a Retreat Centre in the Nile Delta for three months. Jan was the same Jan who came on that trip to Malaysia and then to Thailand. She was the one who sent Thai Bibles to the girls we met at Hat Jai.

Jan had great courage, and stayed without any westerners for company at the Retreat Centre, doing all the hard work one could imagine. She sang, she prayed, she planted, she scrubbed, she cleaned toilets, she cooked, she gardened, she befriended, she listened, she cried, she laughed, she prayed some more, she washed, she hung out, she swept and swept as the desert sand covered everything like a shroud, despite the high walls. During her time there she came to stay with me.

****

I hadn't given much thought to those strange occurrences in and around 9/11. Life became very busy. The world had changed. Which people would come here? And those who did come, how would I care for them, pastorally?

I thought that what I had suspected about Sabry and his sisters was unsubstantiated until I had that 'surprise encounter.'

Just to top up: Jan and I were returning home after a shopping expedition. We turned the corner and stepped into my street. A car on our right came towards us, then suddenly stopped. With a screech of brakes it immediately reversed, speeding up road 315, taking off over the speed bumps. Four wheels in the air!

Night Journeys

'What's happening?' Startled, Jan grabbed my arm.
'It's my old landlord, Sabry. I haven't seen him for ages. One look at me, and he's taken off. Backwards!'
'What's his problem?'
'I don't really know. It's a long story, Jan. I'm still trying to make sense of it. I haven't seen him for ages, until today!'

****

'What do you make of it?' Jan asked as we entered my building.
'I wish I knew'.
I told Jan about that year I lived, with all the other expatriates so happily in Sabry's building. I spoke of the events recorded in this memoir. As I told her all this I realised that I could list all the incidents leading up to 9/11, the disconcerting events after I was the lone tenant in the building, line them up, and find them completely innocuous.
'Now,' I said, 'almost two years after I was turned out of my home by a landlord who seemed to have turned into a monster, I see him. Sabry, white-faced, teeth set, knuckles clenched, eyes staring, driving backwards over the speed bumps like he'd seen a ghost!'
His response to seeing me rattled me, and lots of stuff that I had hidden in the bottom drawer of my subconscious started to emerge from the dark corners.
'What's been happening?' said Jan as she looked around for the tea bags.
'I'm not sure, but when I look back, there seems to be a sequence of strange behaviour. The fashion business that never materialised; a foyer particularly made in pink marble to receive the fashion buyers who never came. An apartment house left to deteriorate; Sabry, never improving the property or making anything of the garden. It was like they were just marking time.'
Jan put on the kettle and I sat at the dining room table a bit shaken and continued with my reminiscences.

'At the end of August, there was the alleged episode with the CIA on the road from Alexandria, and Sabry telling me to leave the next morning. I asked for time to find somewhere else and he granted me that. In early September he flew to Germany again. Then, the day after September 11 2001, he tells me to leave immediately.'

Jan makes us cups of peppermint tea and I continue to speculate. 'Now I feel that we expatriates were a cover for something. We were the perfect cover. No one would suspect a landlord with an apartment filled with westerners as a possible security risk.'

'What do you mean?' Jan's eyes widen.

'Sabry and his sisters were born and bred in Hamburg,' I continue. 'And went to university there. They were neither German, nor Egyptian, and that might have resulted in some discontent. They appeared very uncomfortable in Egypt and I used to wonder why they stayed when they were so isolated and seemingly unhappy in this place.

'Before September 11, Hamburg wasn't on the radar. Only later was it found that the men who flew the planes into the Twin Towers and Washington had met in Hamburg prior to the attacks. Sabry flew to Hamburg regularly. I supposed Sabry had business there; he could be meeting anyone. He and his sisters couldn't have lived on the small rent they got from me.

'The alternative is too terrible to contemplate. Now I'm being forced to contemplate it. Yet, it's all conjecture, assumption and speculation. Where is the evidence of anything criminal?

'What proof do I have?'

****

In January, 2015, the same feelings I had then have resurrected as I conclude this memoir. I have tried to take a sensible approach. I have taken random events in my life with Sabry and his sisters, especially those last two months from the time the tow truck delivered them and their smashed car outside our apartment, to the 9/11 attacks and after, and possibly misconstrued things.

Other explanations to Sabry's changing decisions regarding the use of his building and his tenants could be easily found, and his trips to Germany and in particular to Hamburg could be totally blameless or a coincidence.

All I know is that at the time of 9/11, and then again in January 2003 when Sabry did his 'reverse action' in our street, I did wonder what was really happening. I had no evidence whatever that anything was sinister, except Sabry's blurting out to me on the staircase that they had been run off the road by the CIA. At the time I put that down to his concussion. But the next day he was at my door telling me to leave immediately!

When recounting this to Jan in 2003, I re-awakened fears long buried and that's what I did again – I buried them.

Is it time to dig them up again?

What would an Al Qaeda sleeper cell look like?

What proof do I have?

****

In June 2003 I took a six months Home Assignment. It was a fight to return. In January 2004 I was finally given medical clearance to be allowed back in Egypt for twelve months only. My prayer was to 'finish well' in this place. To leave satisfied that these past 10 ½ years have been a blessed time in the work that God had appointed me to do, work shared by my colleagues, supporters, and friends.

2004, that final year, was made special by my son James coming to stay with me, from January till June. He used his gifts and talents to help Sudanese refugee children find a way of expression and freedom from the ordeals of the past. He used drama, music, art, and poetry. He loved what he did and the Sudanese loved him back.

Raylene Pearce

My health was breaking down. It wasn't discovered till 2006 that my collective symptoms were diagnosed as those of rheumatoid arthritis.

I never saw Sabry or his sisters again.

****

Do you not know? Have you not heard?
The LORD is the everlasting God,
the Creator of the ends of the earth.
He will not grow weary,
and his understanding no one can fathom.
He gives strength to the weary
and increases the power of the weak.
Even youths grow tired and weary,
and young men stumble and fall;
But those who hope in the LORD
Will renew their strength,
they will soar on wings like eagles;
they will run and not grow weary,
they will walk and not be faint.

Isaiah 40 v 28-31

Photo taken by the author on Palm Sunday in Upper Egypt.

Part Seven

Reverse Culture Shock

Chapter Forty Nine

Whachyorname?
(2004)

'Whachyorname? Whachyorname?' Insistent bodies, catching up with their own syncopated chant, surround me on the footpath, wide brown eyes full of mischief.

'Whachyorname? Whachyorname?'

I look at the group of about six ten-year-old boys: *'Ana Raylene men Orstrayla Ganoob'*. I grin and point to my face: *'Ana Si'eedi'*.

The boys roll around with glee. Here is a foreigner who calls herself a *Si'eedi*—a country bumpkin from Southern Egypt. In my case, from Southern Australia!

The boys welcome me with: *'Ah'lan wa sah'lan'*, and then I'm introduced to three Muhammads, two Ahmeds, a Wahid, and a Ramses.

Arriving at the corner of my street, my mob of boys in tow, I catch the eye of a taxi driver and I wave the boys goodbye. I crawl into the back seat of the ubiquitous black and white vehicle, ready for the next conversation that will no doubt include my bona fides and the information that the driver has a cousin in Sydney, actual address unknown.

My anticipation does not disappoint. The taxi driver, Habib, does have a cousin in Sydney and this time he knows what suburb—Lakemba.

****

Night Journeys

Footpaths
(2005)

I have been suffering a collection of symptoms known as reverse culture shock. It is a combination of a feeling of displacement and not-belonging to the culture I once called home. The grief and loss of an ancient and colourful culture that has been my home for a decade permeate every thought.

I am presently privileged to live in a lovely, quiet, and clean southern suburb of Adelaide, but it is in the area of footpaths that I have found my severest challenge.

I have been living in what is termed, in the West, a developing country; however, Egypt has entered its seventh millennium of civilisation, so the word developing is somewhat biased. Australia is not categorised in this way, although as far as the West is concerned, we have only been 'civilised' for a little over two hundred years!

There is much that we can learn from so-called developing countries, and this one particular aspect of Egyptian culture—their footpaths and what happens on them—is where I feel Australia needs help developing.

Where I lived for four years after my return to Australia, in Morphett Vale, the cement footpaths have perfectly sculpted gutters and clay pavers at every corner. As I walked these deserted paths for exercise I felt an intense longing for the people-filled chaotic streets of Cairo.

****

Egyptian Reprise

There is a street I used to walk down each day to work.

The great flame trees, topped with masses of bright red flowers, made a tunnel of lime-green shadows falling onto the uneven dirt footpaths below. At their edges, tightly packed cars, many of them covered with heavy dust-laden tarpaulins, were parked either side of the thin strip of pitted bitumen.

Ahead, the tinkling of bells heralded the presence of the goat lady, her charges chewing everything in sight. Racing between the cars, pouring into hedges and other delectable foliage, twenty or so brown and white noisy goats would halt any other traffic trying to negotiate this narrow avenue.

Invariably, a donkey cart collecting rubbish with young boys brandishing whips to keep them in line would block the corner I planned to turn into. With a nod towards the three soldiers leaning on their AK-47s guarding the corner, I would try to manoeuvre past the animal traffic jam.

The walk to work was only across three streets and three blocks of tenements, but I would greet and be greeted by at least twenty people who regularly marked my journey. These people, whether my friend Ahmed, the florist, or my own doorkeeper, Muhammad, or all the other *boabs*, would know exactly where I was at any given time when asked by the security police.

I never felt lonely on the streets of Cairo.

****

On the other hand, Adelaide is a very tidy city, with streets in neat rows intersecting each other at perfect right angles or, like my street, a neat little cul-de-sac where no one knows me.

There are no goat ladies or donkey carts, no stray camels or packs of yellow, rabid dogs prowling through vacant land between high-risers. With twenty million souls making their homes in huge buildings beside individually made footpaths in Cairo, there is little to compare with the quiet, clean, clinical streets of Morphett Vale.

I'm not suggesting that Australia round up the huge colonies of camels and herds of wild donkeys in the outback to run loose on our streets. But I do feel that our councils could learn a thing or two from

Night Journeys

the incredible footpaths of the great city of Cairo that could be developed to make them more interesting for the local walker and for tourists (both of which abound in Cairo).

****

For example, there is an interesting metal sculpture coiling up in the centre of the footpath just around the corner from my old apartment. (I have no trouble in believing that nothing has changed since I left.) This coil has stood—for at least five years that I know of—about a metre high, covered with some sort of plastic tape that has frayed in the wind to reveal the electrical wires beneath. This structure has always intrigued me and given me cause to think. I have never seen such an interesting piece of artwork on the footpaths of Adelaide.

Next to this artefact is a minute piece of open land covered with a tiny piece of lawn and protected by large bundles of rusty barbed wire. The wire surround sticks out precariously to grab any passer-by who isn't paying attention.

Attention is the operative word here. In lovely Morphett Vale, you can walk for miles along empty footpaths without paying attention to anything. You are unlikely to encounter any barbed wire, and the possibility of being caught up in it is highly improbable.

In the southern suburbs, you can walk along the footpaths and gaze at the clear, unpolluted sky, listen to native birds, admire the neighbours' houses and gardens and never have to look where you are actually putting your feet. This is an element that worries me.

What are we missing out on? Where our feet are placed should be of great interest. Instead, I can walk along my local footpaths completely comatose and possibly missing out on something really important.

****

Like the great expectation of gaping holes! I have always enjoyed peeping into the cavernous potholes that periodically appear in the middle of footpaths in Cairo, just in case something wonderfully ancient, like a mummy, is entombed there. It was my private dream to discover another King Tut or perhaps Alexander the Great's tomb, so footpath walking was full of expectation and exploration.

I can walk for miles in Morphett Vale on immaculate footpaths with no possibility of discovering lost civilisations or a pot of gold.

Another thing that is causing me cultural emptiness is the lack of walled areas alongside footpaths—walls about six feet high where the neighbours can throw their rubbish. This is a very sensible thing to do and you don't have to pay council rates or garbage disposal fees. Eventually, when someone decides to build a multi-storey building there, they won't have to look for any landfill.

Night Journeys

The particular wall that feeds my nostalgia bordered the footpath leading to the front of the office block where I worked. I passed it every day and watched its metamorphosis over several years until it finally collapsed under the weight of millions of tons of compacted garbage. Through the pile of broken bricks I could see layer upon layer of totally squashed rubbish. It's so neat—in the American sense and also in the Australian sense—meaning, tidy.

****

Here, I walk for ages and never see another human being. I never meet anyone. Not even a jogger. In Cairo, you choose to walk down streets filled with people. The more people the better. The more people walking in your street, the safer it is.

****

There is a particular etiquette in walking along footpaths in Cairo that makes it a fascinating experience. As a woman, you never look into men's eyes, otherwise the gentleman coming towards you might abruptly change direction and before you know it, he's coming up behind you, waiting for the invitation that brief eye contact indicated.

In a crowded street, if you were grabbed at, one yell would suffice, and at least a dozen concerned people would surround you, the perpetrator slinking off into the distance, bombarded by a cacophony of indignant voices. I never felt afraid on Cairo streets unless I happened to find myself on a deserted one.

****

This happens all the time in Morphett Vale but doesn't cause me to be afraid, just causes the feeling of living in an un-peopled landscape. And that brings me to another cultural blimp that affected me greatly when I lived in the Middle East: the problem of the emptiness of Australia.

Do you realise that it's impossible to buy a book, calendar, or a magazine about 'Beautiful Australia' that has people in it? And that's a dilemma for an Australian living in a crowded city of twenty million people. My Egyptian friends always asked the embarrassing question as they gazed in wonder at the pristine beaches. 'Where are the people?' So I stopped buying our tourist books.

I just try to take photos that have people in them. Like when I went to Sydney and stood on the Darling Harbour Bridge, which is a purpose-built pedestrian bridge. I waited for half an hour to take a photo with people in it. When I gave that up, I tried to photograph the scene below, where another footpath glistened in the afternoon light and where, in its spotless condition, a half dozen people walked. My son was urging me on, but I insisted in staying there on the bridge as it was already five pm and the crowds should have been there. Finally I clicked my camera and managed to capture the images of fifteen people, walking on the beautiful footpath as wide as a four-lane highway in Cairo.

Finding pedestrians in Australia is a problem. They are all locked up in their shiny cars. Most carry but one person, except those young mothers with children safely tied up in the back seats of 'people-movers'. They drive to the shopping mall, get out of their vehicles, and walk straight into the shops via the underground parking station. Hardly a pair of shoes ever needs to land upon the footpath.

There are those unfortunates who travel by bus or even by our railway system. They manage to avoid the footpaths there too, as many drive to the train stations to go into the city.

One day I took my granddaughter, Holly, then aged seven, to the Adelaide zoo by train. At least that was what we intended to do. But when we got to the Blackwood station we found it shut. This also meant that the toilets were closed and we both needed to go! There was nothing there except closed buildings and a platform with a few forlorn people standing about.

Night Journeys

Anyway, we had to leave the station, walk back through the car park, get into the car, and find a public toilet nearby. We ended up driving all the way to the zoo. Then came the thrill of our lives.

We had the privilege of walking on a footpath!

Admittedly, we didn't have to negotiate coils of electrical wires protruding from the centre of the path, nor did we fall into holes of disintegrating tarmac or bump into poles inconveniently stationed in the middle of the footpath, but, nevertheless, it was a thrill.

We only had to walk about twenty metres, cross a little bridge and enter the zoo. Then for the next three hours we meandered through the enclosures on footpaths especially built so that humans could enter the world of the animals. We really felt as if we were in Malaysia, with the apes swinging from the trees in front of us. No cages, no wires, just we two and a few other humans on elevated footpaths, walking among the exotic birds, and amazing animals.

****

I must tell you what it's like to visit the Cairo zoo. It is totally opposite to the beautiful Adelaide zoo.

For a pound note given to any of the numerous zoo attendants you can feed hunks of grass to hippos, rhinos, gorillas, and any other animal, however dangerous, with a mouth open against the wire enclosures. It's an extreme sport. This feeding is performed while you are beleaguered by hundreds of children calling, 'Whachyorname? Whachyor name?' at the top of their lungs, crowding in and overwhelming you, until the monkey cage seems the best option of escape. Don't go on the weekend or in school holidays if you want to remain in one piece or be left in peace.

Back to footpaths: When you have them, use them! They are meant for feet. In my area of Cairo, there is a group of some forty shops—my local *souk*. In front of the shops, there are forty different forms of footpath at different levels and made from different materials. Sometimes just natural sand, other times highly polished marble from Upper Egypt.

To get to my favourite chicken shop with its cages of live chooks, you have to climb up several marble steps. Then you negotiate a small fountain and several outdoor cooking areas where young lads wave chicken feather fans to keep the fires going.

There is nothing boring about these footpaths. Just keep your eyes on the footpath, watch your step, and don't miss a single moment of the experience. It's all-encompassing! If you don't, then you might disappear down a hole and never be seen again. Totally encompassed!

Many years later you will be excavated and the archaeologists, of whom there are many in Egypt, will make clever deductions as to what dynasty you came from and discuss in great detail the contents of your shopping basket, or as they would probably deduce, burial goods.

Adelaide has a lot of learn from Cairo on how to make innovative, interactively interesting footpaths—also, how to learn to keep your attention on what you are doing, that is, walking from one place to another once you are out of your car. I mean, there are millions of cars in Cairo, but there are twenty million people too, so footpaths are important.

So if you plan on living there—watch out! You almost walked into a newly erected pole wound around with barbed wire with a large rectangular hoarding at head level advertising a new internet company, cleopatra.org, emblazoned on it. As you back away, you almost fall into a recent excavation with a coil of electrical wire inviting you to engage, to interact intimately with it.

That pack of seven yellow dogs coming towards you will run off if you yell loudly and run in their direction waving your arms wildly. The goat lady is very friendly and her charges only eat your vegetables if they aren't safely out of sight in your shopping bag. And the boys with the AK-47s are really nice. I'm not sure if they have been issued with bullets, but it's comforting to have them around, just in case the dogs don't react the way you hope they will.

Night Journeys

Walking past the florist, you will be presented with a red rose and the taxis will stop for you whether you want to go anywhere or not.

As you step off the footpath, make your way steadily across the six-lane highway, moving gracefully between the hundreds of vehicles — cars, trucks, minibuses, big buses, donkey carts, goats, the odd camel, and those jolly dogs. Don't hesitate or you will be run over and people will appear from nowhere and stand you up. From this position, perhaps even with a broken leg or arm, it will be decided whether your injuries are bad enough to involve the driver of the vehicle who was talking to his uncle and forgot to look out the front window at the time of impact.

So it's probably much safer to stay on the footpath, if you can find it, than to wander all over the road, unless you are a local or used to the extreme sport of crossing streets in Cairo. Now isn't that more adventurous and enticing than straight, uninterrupted footpaths in manicured, culturally challenged suburban Adelaide?

****

Chapter Fifty

Home at Last

I drop my hand and she grasps it as she places her tiny feet on the cement footpath.

'This is a beautiful footpath, *Taitah*,' says three-year-old Millie.

I do a double take and ask her why.

'See the beautiful leaf on the beautiful footpath?'

'Yes, I can see the beautiful leaf.'

'And can you see the beautiful stick on the beautiful footpath?'

'Yes I can.'

'And do you see this beautiful crack, *Taitah*?' She balances along the tar-filled fissure. I look down on the light brown head of my granddaughter and think,

'Out of the mouths of babes

...an epiphany!'

Night Journeys

This is a moment to treasure, a moment of returning and accepting my new life. Nothing in Cairo comes close to having Amelia's hand in mine, and her little observations, challenging me to see, to appreciate, and to joyfully re-engage with my own culture.

****

Therefore as God's chosen people holy and dearly loved,
clothe yourselves with compassion, kindness, humility,
gentleness and patience.
Bear with each other and forgive whatever grievances
you may have against one another.
Forgive as the Lord forgave you.
And over all these virtues
put on love, which binds them all together
in perfect unity.

Colossians 3 V 12 – 14

Mark-John, me, Holly, James, Edward and Amelia.
Photo taken by Alison Winter. Christmas 2005

Afterword

The Icing on the Cake

If you are anything like me you love 'love stories'. I want to tell you mine because it's one full of surprises and full of God's grace, his intervention, and guidance. And it will bring you up to date to 2015.

I need to begin in 1979 when a young woman at my church in Coromandel Valley in the Adelaide hills had to leave her philandering husband. I remember sitting with her on the floor in front of her linen press going through her things.

I'd hold up a doily. 'Do you want this?'

'Oh yes', Ruth would say and I'd put it on a pile.

Then I'd hold up a table cloth, 'What about this?'

'That was Phil's Aunty Eileen's present and I've never liked it.'

'Leave it,' said I, and back on the shelf it would go.

Likewise we went through all the cupboards.

Our minister had helped Ruth write the letter to be left on the mantelpiece, and another church family had their truck ready to convey Ruth's modest possessions to her new residence. She was about to commence her midwifery training. When Phil finally returned from his mistress's house with his washing, he'd no longer find his slave waiting. She had done this for eighteen months, her heart breaking. Now she had been released.

A couple of years later Ruth met her Alan and she went to Whyalla to live, to have a wonderful marriage and three lovely children. We kept in touch over the years and I'd stay with her whenever I went to Whyalla on speaking tours while I was working with *The Company*.

In 1984 on Dec 8th my fortieth birthday, my husband divorced me.

Night Journeys

Ruth drove from Whyalla, a five-hour trip, to Coromandel Valley to be with me. She had little David in his car seat and newly born baby Anna-Lisa in the baby cot strapped in the back seat. She wanted to be with me. I didn't know anyone who had been divorced. There seemed to be no one who could identity with me, but 'Little Ruth' came all those long miles to help me through.

A divorce certificate for a fortieth birthday present!

Ruth was my comfort, even as I had been there for her when she finally left that terrible first marriage. My birthday cake was bitter fare, but Ruth made it possible for me to eat it.

For the next twenty-three years I worked for a missionary organisation, *The Company*. After twelve years in the South Australian office, with both boys having grown up and left home, God called me to the Middle East. My friends gave me a lovely 50th birthday party on my 49th birthday with a flower strewn cake. It tasted lovely but it was also a farewell cake with a hint of sadness. I was to leave everyone I knew and loved, to go to the Middle East to work as the Personnel Director with a Christian multi-media company.

I was away for ten years. I travelled the world speaking and preaching in churches, Bible colleges, large conferences, universities, to small groups from the Outer Hebrides of Scotland to Silicone Valley in the United States. My life was full of adventures within and without the volatile Middle East. But you know all that.

I celebrated my sixtieth birthday, with cakes galore in Egypt, bittersweet this time as I was leaving my beloved Egyptians and returning to an unknown future in my home country.

A week after my birthday I returned to Adelaide to start my new 'calling'. I had been accepted into Flinders University as an undergraduate for a degree in English Literature and a minor in Visual Arts. I loved it. I did really well at my studies and was thinking of a future as a writer, and began to do my Honours Degree. The staff liked me and encouraged me in this academic future.

Raylene Pearce

I had pretty well given up on marrying again. Twenty-six years on my own seemed a good basis for living the rest of my life that way. One of my favourite Psalms is Psalm 37 from verse three:

Trust in the LORD and do good;
dwell in the land and cultivate faithfulness.

These two verses I lived out by asking God to use me in any way that suited him. I'd commit the day to him and it was amazing what turned up.

Delight yourself in the LORD

This was very easy to do. To thank him for what he had done for me in Jesus, to thank him for every day of my life, to sing to him at the top of my lungs. This was a delight for me.

And he will give you the desires of your heart.

Looking back on past writings and journaling, I was always asking the Lord for a husband. Earlier on, the main reason was to share the bringing up of my sons, for my sons to be launched into their manhood with a good example of fathering. It didn't happen.

Even when I went as a missionary in the Middle East I was still asking for a husband. Then when I got very busy travelling the world, recruiting people to work for Jesus in the Middle East, I wondered where a husband would fit in my life anyway.

When I got home and began Uni I was still open to the idea, but there was less urgency in it. But in 2008 it was no longer on my list. Some friends still prayed for a husband for me, but he had to be in ministry of some sort and single men who were full-on for God were rare on the ground.

So I got on with my life, cultivating faithfulness, cultivating a garden, cultivating relationships with friends and family and particularly my grandchildren.

My life was full and satisfying. The final lines of this part of the psalm says:

> *Commit your way to the LORD;*
> *trust in him and he will do this.*

So as 2008 got underway, I was busy on my final subjects of my degree and had begun my Honours in Creative Writing. I was attending two tutorials each week, one for Honours students and the other for PhD students and thoroughly enjoying myself. I had a prayer group for missionaries in my home each month and found myself mentoring a number of women from university. And importantly, I had re-settled into life at Coromandel Valley Uniting church.

Meanwhile, in Whyalla a man made an appointment to see a grief counsellor. This man's wife had died of cancer earlier in the year and he had previously endured four and a half years of knowing that she was deathly ill. He had grieved for her for many years and when she died went into a deep grieving for thirty days. He based this on the thirty days Israel grieved for Moses after his death.

He then returned to his work, as the Uniting Church Minister in Whyalla. He thought that he should check up on how he was going so as not to interfere with his role as minister to his congregation. This brought him to '*Good Grief Counselling*'.

After a couple of sessions the counsellor said that he had worked through his grief really well. She suggested that he would marry again.

He said, 'Not for a couple of years.'

She said, 'Why?'

He said, 'It seemed a good length of time.'

She said. 'You have grieved long and hard. Now is the time to think of the future'. Seeing that he was unconvinced she said, 'If you were to consider marrying someone, what sort of attributes would you be looking for in a wife?'

He answered immediately. 'She would need to be more passionate for God than I am and she needs to be creative.'

He went home and prayed, and Raylene Winter came into his mind. He had met her once twelve years before when she spoke in his church and he and his wife had received her prayer letters over the years.

He picked up the recently delivered *Company* magazine, that came three times a year and casually flipped to the centre page and there on the top of the double page article was the name of the writer, Raylene Winter! He read the article and was intrigued to know that she was still enthusiastic for God and that she was creative and more-over she was still Raylene Winter. Maybe she was still single.

A week or so later Greg returned to see Ruth and said that someone had come to mind.

Ruth said, 'I thought as much,' with a knowing look.

In fact he suspected that Ruth might even know her. So he was not going to mention her name. He wasn't sure, but, Raylene may have belonged to the same church Ruth had once attended.

In the middle of the night Ruth woke up and shook Alan awake. 'Greg Pearce is going to marry Raylene Winter!' Alan was not amused.

Something was happening and I was totally oblivious of it. God was doing that circle thing in my life again. He was about to bring back people into my life in ways that only He would have the imagination to do. When you think you have your life all mapped out like I did – things happen. In fact to have a man in my life meant disruption of a very contented life and future as a famous writer and I was not looking to be thus disturbed!

On Sunday afternoon July 6th 2008, I answered the phone.

'Hullo. This is Greg Pearce here. I don't suppose you remember me.'

'Yes, I do,' as I recollected instantly. 'I spoke at your church – Seacliff Uniting - on my first Home Assignment; that would be in 1996 at a Youth Rally. I had just returned from Lebanon. I remember that you and your wife came on my mailing list from then on.'

Greg spoke of the article I had written for *The Company* Magazine, the first one I had written since my return to Australia, four years before! He said he would like to talk to me about it. I invited him to a pumpkin soup lunch the following week.

When Greg came to my door I invited him in saying, 'Come and see my garden'. I love gardening and I soon found out, so did he. We talked for four hours and during that time it was agreed that I would come to Whyalla, at a future date to be organised, to take a Mission at his church.

From the first phone call on July 6th the emails and phone calls became daily events as we arranged the Mission at Whyalla Uniting Church! Even before the Mission happened, something started to change.

Each visit to Whyalla during the following year I stayed with Ruth and Alan. Long ago both Ruth and I knew the extreme agony of rejection. Now we had the men of God's own choosing to partner us in the work of God, wherever that would be. Right now, for both of us, it was Whyalla.

The Sunday after Christmas 2008, the announcement of our pending marriage took place at Coro Valley church to the delight of everyone there.

After 26 years of single-again-ness, I married Greg Pearce at Coromandel Valley Uniting Church on Sat, 18th April 2009. We had three wedding cakes to feed the 400.

Total sweetness.

God used every day of those twenty-six years and all the years before to equip me to be a minister's wife. Now, every day I draw on His grace to be there for Greg and for the others in our church and for our combined families.

So I have my wedding cake. But the Lord had more. He had the icing!

After our marriage we served in Whyalla for nine months. Ruth and I had ministry opportunities together including the Melrose Women's Camp where I was guest speaker. Greg and I had thought it would be another couple of years before Greg's next appointment, but no, the Lord had far more than we could have imagined in store for us.

He'd given me the cake – Greg.

The icing was Coromandel Valley Uniting Church itself!

Greg was called to be their Minister!

He accepted the call and in late January 2010 we moved to Coromandel Valley, back to my church of 34 years.

And now I was returning as their minister's wife!

I had my cake, with the icing like a silver veil flowing down the sides, put in place by my Heavenly Father.

****

Further Acknowledgements

I want to thank Mary May, my dear friend and secretary in Australia, who posted 400+ prayer letters and thank-you notes, four times a year for ten years! For Mark-John Winter who formatted them and for Barry and Gloria Young keeping up the digital mailing list.

And heartfelt thanks for Jean Illman my mentor since 1983. Jean called herself Mum No 2 when she wrote her copious aerograms to me while I was in the Middle East. Jean died on May 10th 2015 on the same date my own mother died forty-three years previously.

Many thanks to my prayer partners who enabled me to travel under the protective canopy of intercession. And my financial supporters, supporting churches, my seconding organization and my home church at Coromandel Valley Uniting, who between them all, facilitated much of the contents of *Night Journeys*.

Special people edited the whole and part of this memoir: I want to acknowledged Berys Nixon, Jill Baker, and Greg Pearce.

Other people edited areas where their stories interconnected with mine. Some remained anonymous and others gave their permission to be named: Ruth and Alan Parker, John and Margaret Beaumont and Mark and Felicity Jaffrey. Thanks to Heather Morley, Barbara Murray, Diana Knights, Jan Fielke, Mary May, Dr Geoff Pike and the Rev Rod James who shared some of this journey with me.

I acknowledge my brother David who survived his big sister's adventures. One final note:

Holly May, in South Australia, and Holly Joy, in Egypt, are now Facebook friends!

****

Raylene Pearce

We are now retired from full-time ministry but still members of Coromandel Valley Uniting Church. Our lives are engaged in being advocates for refugees and asylum seekers, mentors for theological students, and others within the congregation. Together we teach the Bible, write books, and create and maintain our welcoming garden.

We love having friends and family around, especially our five grandchildren, Holly, Edward, Amelia, Eva and Marley.

We thank God for what he has done for us in Christ Jesus.

Night Journeys

****

We always thank God,
the Father of our Lord Jesus Christ,
when we pray for you,
because we have heard of your faith
in Christ Jesus and the love you have
for all the saints -

the faith and love that spring from the hope
that is stored up for you in heaven
and that you have already heard about
in the word of truth, the gospel
that has come to you.

All over the world
this gospel is bearing fruit and is growing,
just as it has been doing among you
since the day you heard it
and understood God's grace in all its truth.

For this reason,
since the day we first heard about you,
we have not stopped praying for you
and asking God to fill you
with the knowledge of his will
through all spiritual wisdom
and understanding.

St Paul writing from prison in Rome to the church at Colosse.

HOW TO SUPPORT PROJECT KOLA

Cheques can be made out to:
Maggie Tucker,
c/- Coromandel Valley Uniting Church,
415 main Rd,
Coromandel Valley 5051

or
Sent directly to:
Project Kola
P.O. Box 231
Bayswater
Victoria, 3153

or
Direct Deposit (from your home PC, iPhone, iPad etc)
To: BSB: 013-225,
Account 2971 14948
In the 'comments/note' space add your name - 1281 – Kola,

This is a project of Coromandel Valley Uniting Church.

Donations over $2 tax deductible.
10% of all royalties for *Night Journeys* will be given to Project Kola.

A young girl washing the dishes in the safety of her own home.

ABOUT THE AUTHOR

Raylene Pearce has written and directed plays, authored magazine articles and worked as a 'mission mobilzer' for twelve years.

In 1994 she was called by God to work in Christian media in the Middle East for ten years. During that time she was a guest speaker on four continents.

In 2008 she obtained a Degree in Creative Writing at Flinders University, Adelaide.

Raylene Pearce now lives with her husband Greg in Coromandel Valley, South Australia.

www.raylenepearce.com

www.ingramcontent.com/pod-product-compliance
Lightning Source LLC
LaVergne TN
LVHW051358080426
835508LV00022B/2873